Beginning JavaScript

The Ultimate Guide to Modern JavaScript Development

Third Edition

Russ Ferguson

Apress®

Beginning JavaScript

Russ Ferguson
Ocean, NJ, USA

ISBN-13 (pbk): 978-1-4842-4394-7   ISBN-13 (electronic): 978-1-4842-4395-4
https://doi.org/10.1007/978-1-4842-4395-4

Managing Director, Apress Media LLC: Welmoed Spahr
Acquisitions Editor: Louise Corrigan
Development Editor: James Markham
Coordinating Editor: Nancy Chen

Cover designed by eStudioCalamar

Cover image designed by Freepik (www.freepik.com)

Distributed to the book trade worldwide by Springer Science+Business Media New York, 233 Spring Street, 6th Floor, New York, NY 10013. Phone 1-800-SPRINGER, fax (201) 348-4505, e-mail orders-ny@springer-sbm.com, or visit www.springeronline.com. Apress Media, LLC is a California LLC and the sole member (owner) is Springer Science + Business Media Finance Inc (SSBM Finance Inc). SSBM Finance Inc is a **Delaware** corporation.

For information on translations, please e-mail rights@apress.com, or visit www.apress.com/rights-permissions.

Apress titles may be purchased in bulk for academic, corporate, or promotional use. eBook versions and licenses are also available for most titles. For more information, reference our Print and eBook Bulk Sales web page at www.apress.com/bulk-sales.

Any source code or other supplementary material referenced by the author in this book is available to readers on GitHub via the book's product page, located at www.apress.com/9781484243947. For more detailed information, please visit www.apress.com/source-code.

Printed on acid-free paper

This space is dedicated to my brother, Rodd, and my Dad.

If not for my Dad, none of this would be possible.
Thanks, Dad.

—Russ

Table of Contents

About the Author

Russ Ferguson is a freelance developer and instructor in the New York City area. He has worked with companies of all sizes, from startups to some of the largest organizations in the world. These companies have spanned industries including cable television, book publishing, finance, and advertising. He has worked on projects for companies like Bank of America, General Mills, LG, Viacom, and DC Comics.

About the Technical Reviewer

Toby Jee is software programmer currently located in Sydney, Australia. He loves Linux and open source projects. He programs mainly in Java, JavaScript, TypeScript, and Python. In his spare time, Toby enjoys walkabouts, reading, and playing guitar.

Acknowledgments

I need to thank everyone at Apress for working with me and keeping me on course to get this book finished. Nancy, Toby, Louise, James, and Jade, thank you.

CHAPTER 1

Introduction to JavaScript

JavaScript has changed a lot over the years. We are currently in a time where there is a JavaScript library for just about anything you would like to build. JavaScript lives both on the client and the server, on the desktop and on mobile devices.

The goal of this book is to help you get an understanding of how the language works, what can be done with it, the resources available, and the some of the ecosystem around the language and tools. At times I will point out things that may be asked on a technical interview, all in an effort to help you get your arms around this growing community. Some of the topics I will cover are

- Understanding JavaScript syntax and structures

- Creating scripts that are easy to understand and maintain

- Using tools to debug JavaScript

- Handling events

- How JavaScript works on the server

- The frameworks that exist to make JavaScript a strongly typed language

- JavaScript application frameworks and how they work

- Retrieving data from the server

JavaScript is essential in modern web development; single page applications (SPAs) make up the majority of sites being created. Understanding JavaScript lets you add interactivity to your website and lowers the learning curve for things like frameworks. This is not to say that you need frameworks for everything, but to add any level of interactivity to your site, you need JavaScript.

© Russ Ferguson 2019
R. Ferguson, *Beginning JavaScript*, https://doi.org/10.1007/978-1-4842-4395-4_1

Enough introduction—you got this book to learn about JavaScript, so let's start by talking quickly about JavaScript on a high level before diving right into it.

In this chapter, you'll learn

- Why JavaScript is important to you as a developer

- How to add JavaScript to a web document

- Object-oriented programming (OOP) in relation to JavaScript

Chances are that you have already come across JavaScript and already have an idea of what it is and what it can do, so I'll move quite swiftly through some basics of the language and its capabilities first. If you know JavaScript well already, and you simply want to know more about the newer and more accessible features and concepts, you may skip a head. However, there may be some information you've forgotten, and a bit of a review doesn't hurt, either.

The Why of JavaScript

As discussed, JavaScript is everywhere. It plus HTML and CSS are all the tools you need to develop a website.

You can work on both the client side and the server using JavaScript. This makes the demand for JavaScript developers very high. And high demand means various job opportunities and competitive rates for developers. As of this writing, the average salary of a JavaScript developer is $110,841 per year in the United States according to Indeed, a job website (www.indeed.com/salaries/Javascript-Developer-Salaries). So not only is JavaScript a language worth taking a look at, it can be a good addition to your toolset a developer. Let's have a quick discussion of what JavaScript is and then move onto writing some code.

What Is JavaScript?

JavaScript is an interpreted scripting language. The host environment will provide access to all the objects needed to execute the code.

The primary example for JavaScript is the ability to add interactivity to a website. This works because the interpreter is embedded into a web browser so you do not need to add any software.

This has made JavaScript a language that is easily accessible because all you need is a text editor and a browser. On the client side, you can add levels of interactivity like responding to button clicks and validating the contents of a form. It will also allow you to take advantage of the APIs (application programming interfaces) that are built into a browser. Adding something like geolocation capabilities to your site is an example of this.

Another use case is to execute JavaScript on the server, using an environment like Node.js. An example of server-side JavaScript is the ability to do things like make requests from a database and respond to HTTP requests and create files.

The majority of this book will focus on the client side; however, there is very little difference from a code perspective.

JavaScript in a Web Page and Essential Syntax

Applying JavaScript to a web document is very easy; all you need to do is use the `script` tag:

```
<script>
  // Your code here
</script>
```

While this is the simplest way of adding JavaScript to the page, it is not recommended. This is an example of inline JavaScript. One of the reasons not to build your site this way is that it becomes hard to maintain over time. Imagine, as your website grows in size, how difficult it would be to keep everything organized.

The preferred way to add JavaScript to an HTML page is to refer to an external `.js` file:

```
<script src="js/myfile.js"></script>
```

Note   HTML 5 requires that the `script` tag have its own closing tag. This will ensure backwards combability with older browsers. In addition, adding the `script` tag right before the ending body tag is considered a best practice.

3

JavaScript Syntax

Learning any programming language is very similar to learning a foreign language. There are rules to follow and that may require a different way of thinking.

There is a lot of problem solving in programming. You spend time looking at a situation and trying to figure out how to use code to solve the problem. With that in mind, let's take that angle in how we discuss JavaScript.

If you want to hold onto a piece of information to be used later, this is called a *variable*. If you remember any high school algebra, there are always examples where a word or letter represents a value:

```
5 + x = 10
```

In this example, x is a variable that represents a number. Using JavaScript, you can declare a variable and give it a value and then use it later:

```
var x = 5;
5 + x = 10;
```

The above code is not perfect JavaScript, but it illustrates the idea of how variables work. The first line uses the keyword var; this is built into the language and can only be used when declaring a variable. At the end of each line is a semicolon, which can be thought of as the period at the end of a sentence. The JavaScript interpreter does not require you to have it. If you do not add semicolons, the interpreter will add them for you. In order to have more control and to make it easier to read, it is recommended that you add them on your own.

The keyword var is not the only way to declare a variable. Other keywords like let and const can also be used. I will cover what makes them different and when one should be used over another in Chapter 3.

Another scenario is when you have some code and you only want to run it when you need it. JavaScript calls this a *function*. You can write a function, add into it all the commands that you want it to execute, and then have it wait until you need it, like so:

```
function doMath(num1, num2){
    let sum = num1 + num2;
    return sum;
}
```

This sample function has the name doMath. This allows the function to be referenced or called from other parts of your code. This function also accepts two arguments or parameters, sum1 and sum2. Think of them as variables for your function; they just represent data that the function will need in order to execute properly. In this case, it's a set of numbers.

Next are the curly braces ({ }). They contain your code block. Everything that you need to make this function work goes here. You can add as many lines of code as you need. As a general rule, a function should perform only one thing. Using doMath as an example, it only adds numbers together. If you want something else to happen, another function should be written. This will help the debugging process. It is also important to note that the JavaScript language itself contains functions to perform things like string manipulation and math.

Let's say you want to leave notes to yourself. In this case, you need to have something in your code that is not going to execute as code. Adding comments to your code can be declared in two variations:

```
// single line comment
```

```
*/
multi line
comment
/*
```

Adding multiline comments is also useful when you are debugging your code. For example, if you do not want to delete what you have, but you do not want the code to execute, you can make it a comment.

So far, you now know how to solve a few problems: how to hold onto data, execute functions, and leave reminders in the code.

Now let's take some time to talk about how the code executes in your browser.

Code Execution

The browser reads the page from top to bottom, so the order in which code executes depends on the order of the script blocks. A *script block* is the code between the <script> and </script> tags; if you have an external .js file, it will also read from top to bottom. (Also note that it's not just the browser that can read your code; the user of

5

a website can view your code, too, so you shouldn't put anything secret or sensitive in there.) There are three script blocks in this next example:

```
<!DOCTYPE html>
<html>
    <head>
        <script type="text/javascript">
            alert("First script Block");
            alert("First script Block - Second Line");
        </script>
    </head>
    <body>
        <h1>Test Page</h1>
        <script type="text/javascript">
            alert("Second script Block");
        </script>
<p>Some more HTML</p>
        <script type="text/JavaScript">
            alert("Third script Block");
            function doSomething() {
                alert("Function in Third script Block");
            }
        </script>
    </body>
</html>
```

If you try it out, you'll see that the alert() dialog in the first script block appears and displays the message

```
First script Block
```

That's followed by the next alert() dialog in the second line displaying the message

```
First script Block - Second Line.
```

The interpreter continues down the page and comes to the second script block, where the `alert()` function displays

```
Second script Block
```

And the third script block follows it with an `alert()` statement that displays

```
Third script Block
```

Although there's another `alert` statement inside the function a few lines down, it doesn't execute and display the message. This is because it's inside a function definition (`function doSomething()`), and code inside a function executes only when the function is called.

So far in this chapter, you've looked at the JavaScript language, seen some of the syntax rules, learned about some of the main components of the language (albeit briefly), and run a few JavaScript scripts. You've covered quite a lot of distance. Before you move onto a more detailed examination of the JavaScript language in the next two sections, let's explore the important parts of the JavaScript language: *functions* and *objects*.

Functions

In the last section, you saw some code that was not executed until you explicitly asked for it. Functions are extremely flexible in JavaScript. They can be assigned to variables and passed as a property to other functions as an argument. Functions can also return another function. Let's take a look at a few examples:

```
var doMath = function(num1, num2) {
        var result = num1 + num2;
         return result;
};

var myResult = doMath(2,3);
```

This example illustrates how you can assign a function directly to a variable and then use that variable to call the function. This function takes two numbers as arguments. When the numbers are passed to the function, they are added together, and the result is returned back to the code that calls the function:

```
function message() {
       return 'It's. the information age ';
}

function displayMessage(msgFunction, person){
   consoe.log(msgFunction() + person) //It's the information age brother!
}

displayMessage(message, "brother!");
```

This example passes a function over to another function. The second function receives a function as an argument and then executes the function inside a `log` command. This function originally called `message` returns a string that will be displayed alongside the string that is also passed inside your `console.log` method.

Functions are a very important part of the JavaScript language, and I will cover them in detail in Chapter 5.

One other concept I will introduce here is the concept of an *object*. I will also go into more detail about objects in Chapter 4.

Objects

Objects are central to the way you use JavaScript. Objects in JavaScript, in many ways, are like objects in the world outside of programming. (It does exist; I just had a look.) In the real world, an object is just a "thing" (many books about object-oriented programming compare objects to nouns): a car, a table, a chair, and the keyboard I'm typing on. Objects have

- **Properties** (analogous to adjectives): The car is *red*.

- **Methods** (like verbs in a sentence): The method for starting the car might be to *turn ignition key*.

- **Events:** Turning the ignition key results in the *car starting* event.

Object-oriented programming tries to make programming easier by modeling real-world objects. Let's say you are creating a car simulator. First, you create a car object, giving it properties like *color* and *current speed*. Then you need to create methods: perhaps a *start* method to start the car, and a *brake* method to slow the car, into which you need to pass information about how hard the brakes should be pressed so that you can determine the slowing effect. Finally, you need to know when something happens with your car. In OOP, this is called an *event*. For example, when the gas tank is low, the car sends a notification (a light on the dashboard) letting you know it's time to fill up. In this code, you will listen for such an event so that you can do something about it.

Object-oriented programming works with these concepts. This way of designing software is now very commonplace and influences many areas of programming—but most importantly to you, it's central to JavaScript programming.

Some of the objects you'll be using are part of the language specification: the `String` object, the `Date` object, and the `Math` object, for example. These objects provide lots of useful functionality that could save you tons of programming time. You can use the `Date` object, for example, to obtain the current date and time from the client (such as a user's device). It stores the date and provides lots of useful date-related functions such as converting the date/time from one time zone to another. These objects are usually referred to as *core objects* because they are independent of the implementation. The browser also makes itself available for programming through objects you can use to obtain information about the browser and to change the look and feel of the application. For example, the browser makes available the `Document` object, which represents a web page available to JavaScript. You can use this in JavaScript to add new HTML to the web page being viewed by the user of the web browser. If you used JavaScript with a different host, a Node.js server, for example, you'd find that the server hosting JavaScript exposes a very different set of host objects because their functionality is related to things you want to do on a web server.

Note   Even though this section covers JavaScript from an object-oriented perspective, the language itself is a multi-paradigm language where you use it as a functional, imperative, or event-driven language.

As you progress through the book, you'll get a more in-depth look at objects: the objects central to the JavaScript language, the objects that the browser makes available for access and manipulation using JavaScript, and your own custom objects. For now, though, all you need to know is that objects in JavaScript are *entities* you can use to add functionality to web pages, and that they can have properties and methods. The Math object, for example, has among its properties one that represents the value of pi and among its methods one that generates a random number.

Summary

In this chapter, you learned about JavaScript at a high level. You learned why JavaScript can be a good tool in your developer toolbox. You also learned some basic syntax and how to add comments to your code. You saw how to use variables to hold onto data for later use and how functions can be used to have code ready on demand. Another subject was code execution (how the browser reads code from top to bottom). The largest section was the discussion of objects. If you are going to work with JavaScript either on the client or on the server, it is important to understand that working with objects is at the core of JavaScript.

Next, you will take a look at some of the tools you, as a JavaScript developer, have available to you.

CHAPTER 2

JavaScript and Development Tools

There is a lot to get your head around if you are new to developing JavaScript applications. A question often asked is "Where do I start?" This is the goal of this chapter, to help you locate resources and tools that can help you on the path to developing applications with JavaScript. I will also go over some basic usage of these tools. This chapter is not designed to be a definitive guide or as product placement, but it should point you in the right direction.

Here are a few subjects I will go over in this chapter:

- Tutorials and resources
- Integrated development environments (IDEs)
- A quick introduction to Node.js and npm
- Git and GitHub

Tutorials and Resources

There are a lot of websites you can use to gather information about JavaScript, HTML, and CSS. Here are some of the more useful sites:

- MDN web docs at `https://developer.mozilla.org/en-US/docs/Web/JavaScript`
- Free Code Camp at `www.freecodecamp.org/`
- Khan Academy at `www.khanacademy.org/computing/computer-programming/html-css-js`

© Russ Ferguson 2019
R. Ferguson, *Beginning JavaScript*, https://doi.org/10.1007/978-1-4842-4395-4_2

11

- Atlassian's tutorial on Git at `www.atlassian.com/git/tutorials`

- Node.js and the Express framework at `https://developer.mozilla.org/en-US/docs/Learn/Server-side/Express_Nodejs`

These sites were chosen because they offer good information and are free. There are other sites that offer excellent information. Egghead.io (`https://egghead.io/`) provides some free tutorials and also a subscription service. I also recommend the sites Front End Masters (`https://frontendmasters.com/`) and Pluralsight (`www.pluralsight.com`).

Integrated Development Environments

An IDE is the software you use to edit your code. Some editors are made to work with any language by using extensions. Others are made to optimize the experience of one type of language. Like browsers, there are many editors to choose from.

A popular and free choice is Visual Studio Code (`https://code.visualstudio.com/`). It provides everything you need to edit HTML, JavaScript, and CSS, as well as other languages.

Other editors include

- WebStorm (`www.jetbrains.com/webstorm`)

- Brackets (`https://brackets.io/`)

- Sublime Text (`www.sublimetext.com/`)

These tools will help you develop any type of software application. Features they commonly possess are

- **Autocomplete**: An IDE figures out how to complete the line of code you are writing.

- **Debugging tools**: You can do things like watch the values of variables from inside the IDE.

- **Inline command line interface**: The IDE lets you perform operations on the command line. This is useful for things like working with node modules and version control systems like Git.

- **Extendable**: They have the ability to add features that let you edit in languages other than the basic HTML, CSS, or JavaScript.

If you have Visual Studio Code (Figure 2-1) installed, you can make a simple HTML page that you can use for the rest of this exercise.

Figure 2-1. *Visual Studio Code is an source code editor that runs on Windows, MacOS, and Linux*

Create a folder anywhere on your computer, and then open that folder in your editor. You are going to make your first HTML page. As you go through the examples in this chapter, you will set this folder up as a local web server.

I won't go into all the details of how HTML works; for this exercise, I will give you a quick template. This should be enough to get you going.

Control-N (Command-N if you are using MacOS) will open a new file. Add the following code to your document:

```
<!DOCKTYPE html>
    <html lan="en">
        <head>
                <meta charset="utf-8">
                <title>Chapter 2</title>
                 <body>
        <p>Hello World</p>
                </body>
        </head>
    </html>
```

Save it as `index.html`. This is your first page. At the moment you can drag and drop this into your browser. This is not the same as having it served to you as if you were getting it from the Web. That's ok because you are going to fix that in the next section.

Node.js

This is going to be a very high-level introduction to Node.js. In future chapters, you will go into some use cases that will display the power of this tool.

Node is an open-source JavaScript environment that allows you to execute JavaScript on the server side. This gives you the ability to use the same language to run code both on the client and now the server.

Node uses a collection of modules. Modules make up the core functionality of Node and allow you do to things like work with the file system, with network protocols (HTTP, DNS, etc.), binary data, and the ability to talk to database.

The quickest way to get Node is directly from the website (`https://nodejs.org/`). Once on the site, download the version described as "Recommended For Most Users" (at the time of this writing, it's 8.11.3). Once installed, you are one step closer to setting up your folder from the last example as a web server.

Node does not have a GUI. To use it, you need to get used to working with the command line. There aren't a lot of commands in this example. Here are the things that you are going to do:

- Download a module called http-server that lets you serve your folder as if it was coming from a web server.

- Navigate to your folder with the source code and use the module to launch your site and look at it in the browser.

Most IDEs have a terminal emulator built in. If you are using Visual Studio Code, go to View and then choose Integrated Terminal. This will be your command line interface for your project.

The first thing you want to do is make sure that Node has been installed. At the prompt, type

```
node -v
```

This should return the version number of Node, as shown in Figure 2-2. If this is not working, make sure that Node is installed.

```
Russs-MacBook-Pro-2:~ asciibn$ node -v
v10.4.1
Russs-MacBook-Pro-2:~ asciibn$
```

Figure 2-2. *Visual Studio Code has a built-in terminal that lets you execue commands*

If everything is good, install the module, as shown in Figure 2-3. This is using Node Package Manager. The package manager is a way of organizing libraries of code. It may contain utilities like this or other libraries like Angular to help build your project.

Figure 2-3 shows the results of loading the node module. Let's go over the first line since that is what you need to do to get this to work. Node Package Manger commands start with npm. To install a module, tell npm the name of the module you want to install. If you want that module to work anywhere on your computer, add -g.

```
Russs-MacBook-Pro-2:~ asciibn$ npm install -g http-server
/usr/local/bin/http-server -> /usr/local/lib/node_modules/http-server/bin/http-server
/usr/local/bin/hs -> /usr/local/lib/node_modules/http-server/bin/http-server
+ http-server@0.11.1
added 25 packages from 28 contributors in 3.469s
Russs-MacBook-Pro-2:~ asciibn$
```

Figure 2-3. *Install the module http-server. It lets you use any folder on your hard drive as a local server.*

One of the nice things about having the command line interface built into the IDE is that it knows exactly which folder you are working in. So now you can have your module turn the folder into a local web server. Type in this command:

```
http-server
```

You should see something like Figure 2-4.

```
Russs-MacBook-Pro-2:code asciibn$ http-server
Starting up http-server, serving ./
Available on:
  http://127.0.0.1:8080
  http://192.168.100.6:8080
Hit CTRL-C to stop the server
```

Figure 2-4. *Running the http-server module to make any folder on your hard drive a local webserver*

With a few short steps you now have the ability to make that folder on your hard drive serve up the HTML page. The two numbers you are looking at are your IP (Internet Protocol) address to your folder. The first one is always your machine. The second number is an address on your network. This is useful if anyone on your network wants to see what you are working on.

After the colon there is a set of numbers. In Figure 2-4, it is 8080, which is the port on the network that the HTML page is being served though. Data can be sent or received to the server though different ports. This number, 8080, is frequently used. Future examples will show HTML data being served from different ports.

You can control-click either address and your browser should open and show you the page shown in Figure 2-5.

Hello World

Figure 2-5. *Looking at the results of running the http-server module in a browser. You can serve HTML pages.*

With your new setup, you now have a way to create and edit HTML, JavaScript, and CSS. Using Node, you can take any project folder on your hard drive and turn it into a local server. This gives you some important tools for a modern front-end developer workflow.

Now comes the question of keeping track of your code. As you make updates to your site and add more files, a good practice to get into is to keep track of the changes you make. This is more than just doing an "undo" if you have a problem. Imagine you add features to the site and then later realize you need to back it up to a previous state. Version control is important for projects, even more so when you have more than one person working on them.

In the next section, I will talk about Git and sites like GitHub and Bitbucket.

Version Control Systems

Using any type of version control system is a good idea. Projects grow and change over time and it is good to get a "snapshot" of the project. Git has become a popular way to accomplish this. In this section, you will

- Install Git.

- Use Git to track your file.

- Create an account with GitHub.

- Upload your project to GitHub.

Git is easy to install. Go to `https://git-scm.com/`. You can install it for whatever operating system you are working on. The site offers resources for learning how Git works. The free eBook can be found at `https://git-scm.com/book/en/v2` and other tutorials can be found at `https://try.github.io/`.

This is another tool that does not have a UI. Similar to Node, you use the command line to move around. There are some tools that you can use that will help out. Sourcetree is a free tool that can help you work with Git (`www.sourcetreeapp.com/`). The examples in this chapter will continue to use the command line.

Note   If you are running Windows, after installing Git you may have something extra installed called Git Bash. This tool emulates the kind of commands on Unix or MacOS. It is really the same thing as the integrated editor. The only difference is that is it a separate application. For now, just stay with your integrated terminal.

If you have your IDE open, return to the terminal. The first thing to do is make sure that Git has been installed. A quick way to do so is to see what version is installed. Inside the terminal, type

```
git -version
```

Similar to checking for the version of Node, this will return the version of Git that is currently installed.

Once you've confirmed that Git is installed and running, you can initialize the folder to work with Git. You do it this way:

```
git init
```

This will set up your folder to work with Git. By creating an invisible folder called .git (you can change your folder settings to see it), Git will be able to track not just the files but the contents of the files over time.

Now you can check the status of the files and see if they are being tracked or not. At the command line, type

```
git status
```

This should now output the status of your project (Figure 2-6).

```
Russs-MacBook-Pro-2:code asciibn$ git status
On branch master

No commits yet

Untracked files:
  (use "git add <file>..." to include in what will be committed)

        index.html

nothing added to commit but untracked files present (use "git add" to track)
Russs-MacBook-Pro-2:code asciibn$
```

Figure 2-6. *Git uses a branching model. The current branch is master. In this instance, index.html is not being tracked by Git. For a full tutorial on Git, refer to the "Tutorials and Resources" section.*

At this point, Git is not tracking your file. If you want to change that, type

`git add index.html`

See Figure 2-7.

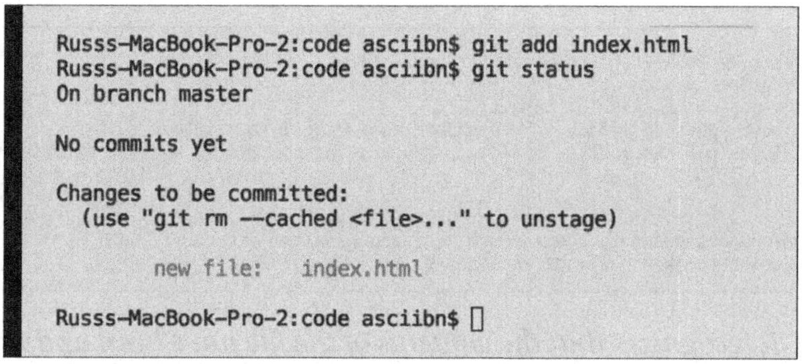

```
Russs-MacBook-Pro-2:code asciibn$ git add index.html
Russs-MacBook-Pro-2:code asciibn$ git status
On branch master

No commits yet

Changes to be committed:
  (use "git rm --cached <file>..." to unstage)

        new file:   index.html

Russs-MacBook-Pro-2:code asciibn$ []
```

Figure 2-7. *Git now knows it needs to track index.html.*

This tells Git to keep track if this file, so now if there are any changes to the contents of the file, Git will know about it. Making sure that Git knows what to track is important. Also important is to make commits. Think of them as snapshots of what is going on with your files at any given time.

At the command line, type

`git commit -m "my first commit"`

Take a look at Figure 2-8. You are asking Git to perform a commit and adding the `-m` flag. This allows you to add a message about the commit you are about to make.

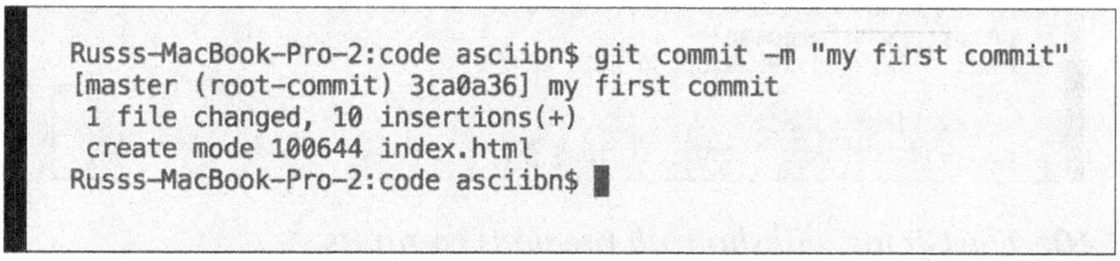

```
Russs-MacBook-Pro-2:code asciibn$ git commit -m "my first commit"
[master (root-commit) 3ca0a36] my first commit
 1 file changed, 10 insertions(+)
 create mode 100644 index.html
Russs-MacBook-Pro-2:code asciibn$ 
```

Figure 2-8. *Creating a snapshot of the file using the git commit command*

All of this is local to your machine. Git is aware that the file is being modified. If you make any change to the current document, for example, if you change the message, Git will be aware of it. Make a change, save the file, and then check the status again. See Figure 2-9.

```
Russs-MacBook-Pro-2:code asciibn$ git status
On branch master
Changes not staged for commit:
  (use "git add <file>..." to update what will be committed)
  (use "git checkout -- <file>..." to discard changes in working directory)

        modified:   index.html

no changes added to commit (use "git add" and/or "git commit -a")
Russs-MacBook-Pro-2:code asciibn$
```

Figure 2-9. *Git recognizes that the contents of the file have been updated*

Now that the file is different, you can add the file again and make a new commit. All these commits are kept in a log. If you want to see the history of commits, type

`git log`

Figure 2-10 shows the history of this branch. Each commit comes with a hash number, author, and date/time of when the commit was made.

```
Russs-MacBook-Pro-2:code asciibn$ git log
commit c7f65e3407bbdc75941b7744a4774403906957d6 (HEAD -> master)
Author: Russ Ferguson <                      >
Date:   Sat Jun 23 21:51:59 2018 -0400

    my second commit

commit 3ca0a36528157b57461778767ddab9e8f456782f
Author: Russ Ferguson <                      >
Date:   Sat Jun 23 20:50:40 2018 -0400

    my first commit
Russs-MacBook-Pro-2:code asciibn$
```

Figure 2-10. *The Git log will show all previous commits*

In Figure 2-10, you can see that when adding a message to your commit, you really should be more descriptive than what you see here. The message can give you a good idea of what is going on without looking into the code.

At this point, you can create a repository in Git. Add a file to be tracked and make multiple snapshots of that file. As mentioned, all of this is local to your machine, which is fine if you are working by yourself. What if you are working with other people? Then you need a server to not only host your code but to keep track of the changes. This is where sites like GitHub and Bitbucket come in.

For your purposes, these sites do the same thing. They are a place to host code. The repository you create can either be public or private.

As the name suggests, the public repositories are available for anyone to see, download, or clone. People can also contribute to the project by sending changes and bug fixes.

GitHub (recently acquired by Microsoft at the time of this writing) allows public, private, and open source repositories for free. Bitbucket has unlimited private repositories for free for small teams (up to five users).

You can sign up to either of these sites. The screenshots for this section will be using GitHub. Once signed in, you can make a new repository. This will be a public repo. You can see that it is attached to your account (Figure 2-11).

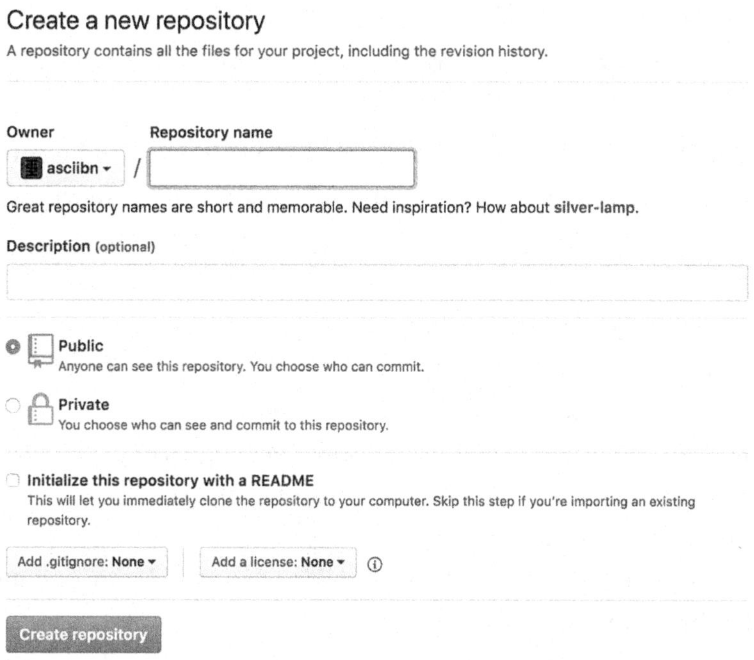

Figure 2-11.   Creating a new repository on GitHub

Once the repo has been created, you will get instructions on how to connect your local machine to the repo. Name this example as MyFirstProject (Figure 2-12).

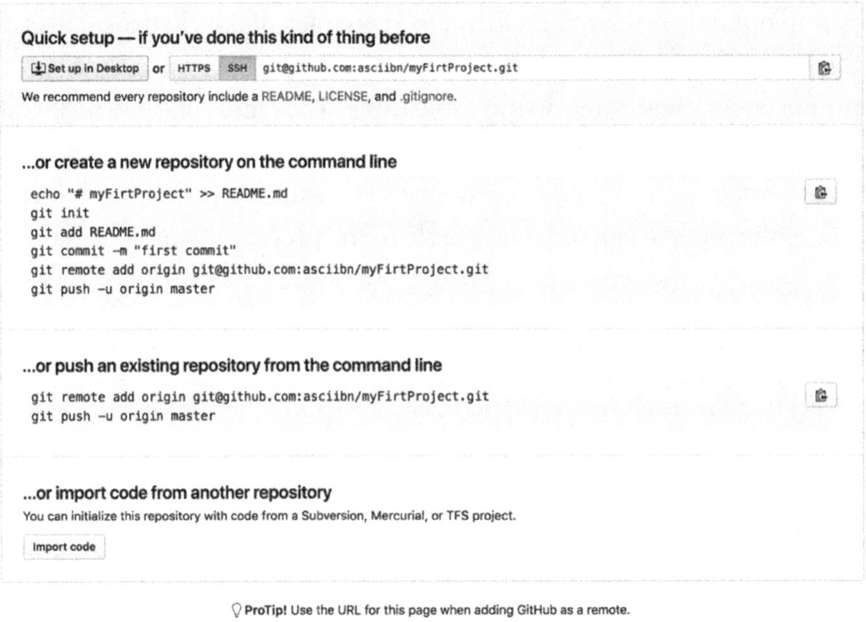

Figure 2-12. *Instuctions on how to connect your local repo to GitHub*

The README.md file is the file you update when you want people who come to the repo to know what the project is about. When you first come to a project, any notes about how it was made, how to get it installed, and what technology was used are usually in the README file.

If you went over the section on Git, these commands should be familiar. The initialization of the project and adding the README file should be familiar from that section. What is new here is the addition of the remote function.

Git uses a concept called *remotes*; these remotes are copies of your files on a server. This will let you push (or upload) your files to a remote source.

You may notice -u in the example. It sets the default location of the remote branch. In the future, when you try git pull, this will pull (or download) any updated versions of the code from the remote server.

Once you tell your local Git instance where the remote is, then the next command is to push your files to the server.

All of these commands can be executed back in the terminal window in your IDE or GitBash if you have it installed.

The code that is pushed to the remote repo does not give you a functional website. Remember that these services are for tracking changes in your code over time and do not show the results of what your website does.

Once you push your code to the repo, you can then inspect the site (Figure 2-13).

```
Enter passphrase for key '/Users/asciibn/.ssh/id_rsa':
Enter passphrase for key '/Users/asciibn/.ssh/id_rsa':
Enumerating objects: 6, done.
Counting objects: 100% (6/6), done.
Delta compression using up to 8 threads.
Compressing objects: 100% (4/4), done.
Writing objects: 100% (6/6), 582 bytes | 582.00 KiB/s, done.
Total 6 (delta 1), reused 0 (delta 0)
remote: Resolving deltas: 100% (1/1), done.
To github.com:asciibn/myFirtProject.git
 * [new branch]      master -> master
Russs-MacBook-Pro-2:code asciibn$ █
```

Figure 2-13. *Using the command-line to push the current local project to GitHub*

Note   When trying to push your code to the server, you may be asked for your password. It's the password for the account you just created. Once entered, everything will work.

If you get tired of adding your password every time, you can set Git up to remember your password. Go to `https://help.github.com/articles/ caching-your-github-password-in-git/` to set Git up for the operating system you are using.

As shown in Figure 2-14, GitHub will show all the information that is known about your project. This gives you a visual reference and a way to control updates if you ever decide that you want to have an open source project. All the same information is also available to you if you make a private repository.

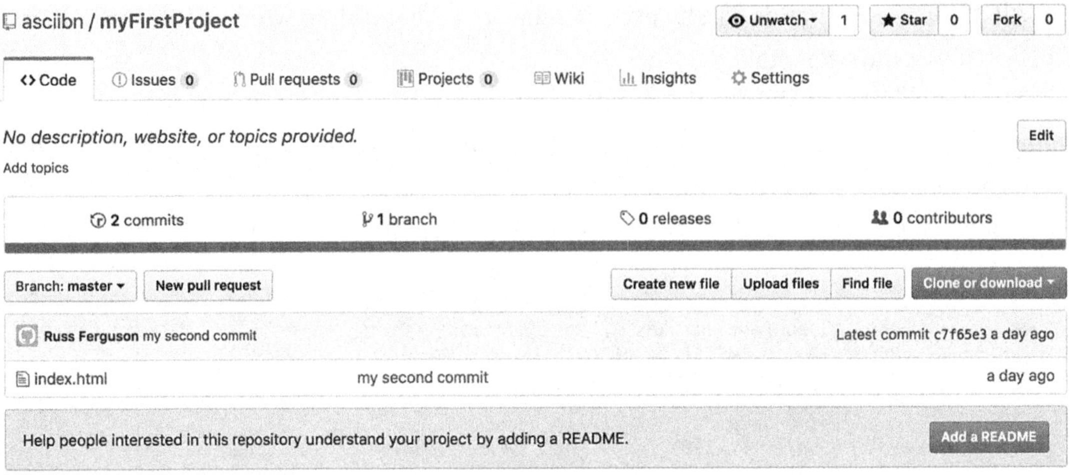

Figure 2-14. *A working public repoistory on GitHub*

Summary

You worked on a lot in this chapter. So far, you picked an IDE, set up version control, and even created a remote repository to work with. The only thing missing is a live site that you can show people. Chapter 13 is where you will build a working site that can be deployed to a live server.

Now, with all the development tools installed and set up, you can dig into the language and make the browser work for you. The next chapter will cover how JavaScript deals with data types.

CHAPTER 3

JavaScript Variables

In this chapter, you will learn some basic JavaScript data types. When you want the computer to hold onto some information, that information is of a certain "type." For example, an email address is a type called String. The computer recognizes that your email address is a series of letters, numbers, and symbols.

If you want to perform a calculation, the computer will consider the data that you are using to perform that calculation as a number. It can calculate numbers but not strings.

As you go through the chapter, you will explore some of these data types. In addition you will also see how variables work.

In this chapter, I use the term "environment;" it simply means where the JavaScript is being executed, which could be either in the browser or using Node.js.

Declaring Variables in JavaScript

JavaScript is a loosely typed or dynamic language. This just means that JavaScript is very accommodating to you. Depending on how you feel about this, this could be good or bad. When you want the environment to hold onto a value, you must declare a variable.

If you create a variable and assign it a value, you can then change that value for something that is completely different. Let's see that in action (Figure 3-1).

```
> var userName = "Violator"
< undefined
> userName = 42
< 42
> console.log(userName);
  42
< undefined
> |
```

Figure 3-1. Using the console in Chrome to test JavaScript variables

© Russ Ferguson 2019
R. Ferguson, *Beginning JavaScript*, https://doi.org/10.1007/978-1-4842-4395-4_3

25

Open your web browser, find the developer tools, and go to the console. When you are in the console, type in the code from Figure 3-1. Set the value of `userName` to `"Violator"`; you can see it's in quotes, which makes it a string. Then it is reassigned to the number 42, which has no quotes around the characters, so it is considered a number.

JavaScript allows for different ways of declaring variables. There are some rules that you need to follow.

When creating a variable, you first need to let the environment know that this is your intention. Here I will introduce the idea of keywords.

The keyword you will use for this example is `var` (short for variable). This keyword will tell the environment that you want to hold onto some information.

There are other keywords built into JavaScript that will let the environment know how to work with things like dates, numbers, and even the HTML document currently inside the browser. You will explore them in future examples.

Here you are creating a variable called `userName`. This capitalization is called *camel case*, where the first letter of every other word has a capital letter. It's not the only way to create variables but you will see it often.

When naming variables in JavaScript, you cannot start with a number or a symbol (consider characters like @ a symbol). All variables can start with a letter; it does not matter if it is upper or lower case. Any character after that can use numbers or symbols. Variables also cannot have spaces in the name. Look at the examples in Listing 3-1.

Listing 3-1. Valid and Invalid Ways to Create a Variable

```
var  user name = "Violator"; // not a valid variable
var !username = "Violator"; // not a valid variable
var 1user_name = "Violator"; // not a valid variable
var user_name = "Violator"; // valid variable
var userName = "Violator"; // valid variable
var username = "Violator"; // valid variable
```

This is not an exhaustive list of how variables are named, but it should give you an idea of how naming variables in JavaScript should work.

Note   For a more exhaustive list, take a look at *JavaScript Recipes*, also published by Apress.

Once you tell the environment that you need to hold onto some information, the next thing is to assign data to that variable. That data is of a certain type. In this example, you assigned the string "Violator" to your newly created variable.

Strings are a representation of data that can be used in text form. Things like the contents of an email, user names, and passwords are all strings. When creating a string variable in JavaScript you can use either single or double quotes around the characters you want to use. The important thing is to be consistent. You cannot start with a single quote and end with a double quote or the other way around.

Using quotes around your characters is important because there is a difference between having "1" (the number in quotes) or 1 (just the number) assigned to a variable. The first is a string; the second is a number. Numbers are a different data type in JavaScript. This is also true with symbols; "@" is considered a string.

At the end of each statement is a semicolon. This is like the period at the end of a sentence. If you do not add one, the environment is good at trying to figure out what you mean and will insert one where it thinks it's necessary.

One of the problems you may run into is when the environment inserts the semicolon in the wrong place. This will create errors during runtime.

However, it does make your code easier to read if you add it. So, as a best practice, add semicolons to the end of each statement.

In summary, when declaring variables in JavaScript, use a keyword (in this case var), name your variable, and then assign its value.

Reassigning Variables in JavaScript

Some variables in JavaScript can be reassigned. This means, once you give a variable a value, it is easy and, in some cases, necessary to go back to that variable and give it a totally new value.

An example of updating an existing variable in JavaScript is if you are tracking whether a user has access to something. You can use a variable as a flag to check someone's status. Here is an example:

```
if ( hasAccess === true ){
    hasAccess = false;
}
```

This example illustrates the idea that a variable can have more than one value. The variable `hasAccess` can have a value of true or false and here you use an `if` statement to check the *current* value.

Using true or false as values makes your variable a Boolean datatype, meaning that it should only have one value or the other. Booleans can only be true or false.

There may be times where you need a variable to have a constant value. The keyword in this case is `const`. At no time do you want the value of this variable to change. Let's see an example.

Variables That Can't Be Reassigned

What if you have data that should not be changed? In this case, you want a variable that can contain a value that will stay constant no matter what else is going on. JavaScript provides such a variable type and it's called a *constant*.

Constants are a type of variable where you cannot change the value after first assigning it. Figure 3-2 shows an example of trying to change the value of a constant.

```
> const userName = "Violator"
< undefined
> userName = "Exciter";
⊗ ▶ Uncaught TypeError: Assignment to constant variable.
      at <anonymous>:1:10
> console.log(userName)
  Violator
< undefined
> |
```

Figure 3-2. *Variables labed a constant can't be changed after first given a value*

Using the keyword `const` will let you do the same thing as using `var`, with the difference being that you cannot reassign the value later. In the example in Figure 3-2, you see that the browser throws an error.

While you cannot reassign a single value to a constant, if you were to assign an object, the properties of that object can be updated. Listing 3-2 contains an example.

Listing 3-2. Assigning an Object to a Constant

```
const myObj = {}
myObj.firstName = "Vince"
console.log(myObj)
{firstName: "Vince"}
  myObj.lastName = "Clarke"

console.log(myObj)
{firstName: "Vince", lastName: "Clarke"}
myObj = {}
Uncaught TypeError: Assignment to constant variable.
```

Since the constant is an object, you can access the properties of that object and update them. I will fully address the concept of an object in next chapter. For now, think of an object like a noun.

This "thing" has properties, (height, width, color, etc.). The *properties* of the object (this "thing") *can* be updated. But the variable myObj cannot be reassigned. In the last line you can see that the browser will throw an error when trying to reassign a new value to the object.

Up to this point I've discussed the ability to create a variable, assign values to it, and update it. I showed instances where you cannot assign a new value to a variable.

The next section will go over how the environment can control the reach, context, or "scope" of a variable.

Variables That Can Only Be Used in a Single Code Block

Let's first define a *code block*. When you work with JavaScript functions, you will often see a set of curly braces ({}). This is your code block. Anything inside these braces is code that will be executed. When using the keyword let to declare your variables, the browser understands that the value that you are assigning to the variable can only be seen inside that block. Listing 3-3 contains an example.

Listing 3-3. A let Statement Only Has a Value While Inside the Code Block

```
for (let i = 0; i < 10; i++) {
  console.log(i); //output = numbers between 0 and 9
}

console.log(i) //error i is undefined
```

Here you have a loop. It creates a variable called i and starts with a value of 0, and as long i does not have a value of 10, it adds 1 to i.

While this loop is happening, you print out in the console the current value of i. This will show values 0 to 9 (as long as the value is less than 10).

All of this is happening inside the curly braces. Once this loop is finished, the variable i goes away. The environment does not think about it anymore. So, when you try to reference that variable in the very next line, it will throw you an error.

So, to recap, as the code is being executed within the curly braces, the variable being used has a value. When the block has finished executing all of the code, the variable is no longer accessible to other parts of your code. It no longer exists.

This is one of the major differences between let and var. Listing 3-4 shows a similar example using var.

Listing 3-4. A var Statement Will Retain Its Value After the Code Block Has Been Executed

```
for (var i = 0; i < 10; i++) {
  console.log(i); //output = numbers between 0 and 9
}

console.log(i) //returns 10
```

If var behaved like let, you would get the same result, where the value of i would return undefined. Instead, the loop behaves exactly the same, but in this case your variable *is* accessible outside the loop and prints out the value of 10.

Variables created with the var keyword are declared based on its current execution context. In the first instance, the loop is not inside a function; because of this, the variable becomes global in scope.

Right under that you have the same loop, but this time it's inside a function block. The variable then is inside a different execution context. If you try to print the value of the variable *outside* the function, the browser will throw an error. See Listings 3-5 and 3-6.

Listing 3-5. When Creating a Variable with the var Keyword, It Will Exist Inside the Current Execution Context. The Code Here Is Outside a Function, Making the Context Global.

```
for (var i = 0; i < 10; i++) {
        console.log(i); //output = numbers between 0 and 9
}

console.log(i) //returns 10
```

Listing 3-6. When Creating a Variable Using the var Keyword Inside a Function, the Execution Context is Local to the Function

```
function goLoop(){
   for (var i = 0; i < 10; i++) {
        console.log(i); //output = numbers between 0 and 9
   }
}
goLoop();
console.log(i) //returns error
```

When working with variables, using let over var will make sure that variables exist only inside the code block that you create. The reason why variables behave differently is because of *variable hoisting*. The next section will explain hoisting in more detail.

Interview Question   What is the difference between var, const, and let? Name some JavaScript data types.

Variable Hoisting

During interviews you may be asked about variable hoisting. It sounds much more difficult than it is. This section will clear up any confusion about how it works.

When the browser is going through its *compile* phase, it will put both functions and variable *declarations* into memory.

Here is an example of how you declare a variable:

```
userName = "Stephanie";
```

31

This is different than when you initialize a variable using one of the keywords like `let`. Here you are assigning a value to a variable and not using any keywords. Because no keyword has been assigned to this variable, it is considered a global variable. It's the same as using the `var` keyword.

This next example shows working code even though it does not look like it should work:

```
userName = "Stephanie";
console.log(userName); //returns Stephanie
var userName;
```

While it looks like the result should be `undefined`, it returns the correct value. Similar to other examples, you use the keyword `var` where the scope or execution context is not set to a code block.

Variables that are hoisted move to the top of the current scope. So, if there are no functions, variables are moved to the global scope. If a variable (using the `var` keyword) is declared inside a function, it would move to the top of that scope.

Variable hoisting takes effect when the variable has been declared, *not* when it has been assigned a value. If you declare a variable without a value, it is still hoisted even if it does not have a value. Listing 3-7 contains an example.

Listing 3-7. Variables Are Hoisted When They Are Declared, Not When They Are Assigned a Value. These Two Examples Produce the Same Result.

```
function checkVars(){
   console.log(username); //returns undefined
   var username = "Hunter";
   console.log(username); //returns Hunter;
}
checkVars() //executes function;

function checkVars(){
   var username;
   console.log(username); //returns undefined
   username = "Hunter";
   console.log(username); //returns Hunter;
}

checkVars() //executes function;
```

Interview Question   What is hoisting and how does it work?

Strict Mode

Strict mode tells the browser to run a more restricted version of JavaScript. This is something you can opt into. Running your code in strict mode will keep the browser from making mistakes that make it difficult to optimize the code.

It will also prevent some syntax from being executed when that syntax will likely be added to a future version of JavaScript. It also eliminates silent errors (errors without feedback from the browser).

You can invoke strict mode on the whole JavaScript file or on individual functions. To add it to the entire script at the top, add use strict; to your code.

In Listing 3-8, if you declare a variable without initializing it, the browser will throw an error.

Listing 3-8. Variables Declared While in Strict Mode Must Be Initalized

```
x = "think tank" //Reference Error: x is not defined
```

This is true if you try to assign an object to a variable that has not yet been initialized:

```
X = {user:"Player One", score:1000} //Reference Error: x is not defined.
```

Individual functions can run in strict mode just by adding the same line inside the body of the function. See Listing 3-9.

Listing 3-9. Using "use strict" Inside a Function Declaration Will Tell the Browser to Run Just That Function in Strict Mode

```
function myFunction(){
   "use strict";
 // add commands here
}
```

Using strict mode ensures that the browser will execute your code in the most efficient way possible and give you the most amount of feedback when errors occur.

Summary

This chapter covered how variables are created and when you should use a certain type of variable. Some variables live inside a code block and others cannot be updated.

You explored the concept of variable hoisting. When using the keyword var, variables can then be hoisted or moved to the top of the execution context. This can cause situations where even though a variable has been declared, it may not yet have a value and so will return undefined as a value.

The last section introduced some of the benefits of running your code in *strict mode*. It will execute a more efficient version of JavaScript and give better feedback by returning errors when the browser may otherwise ignore them.

The next chapter will go into more detail about how objects work and introduce a certain kind of object called an *array*.

CHAPTER 4

JavaScript Objects and Arrays

The last chapter introduced variables. Using variables, you can save information to use later. As applications become more complex, the ability to remember user settings, URLs, or the contents of a form becomes more important.

One of the problems that you run into with a variable is, no matter the type, you can only hold onto one piece of information at a time. If you assign a new value to a variable, the original value is gone. This prevents you from holding onto complex types of data.

It is also not reasonable to create a large number of variables for the purpose of simulating something complex. For example, if someone is filling out a form, it would be hard to manage all the individual variables for each item in the form.

Objects are a great way to group data. Objects are also used in JavaScript to help you perform operations in your application.

The document object is a good example of this. It lets you explore the HTML page that is inside your browser.

The Math object can help perform mathematical operations, while the Date object will let you retrieve not only the current date but help calculate dates in the past or the future. It can also help you put that date in the correct format.

This chapter will discuss what a JavaScript object is, how objects work, and explain what properties and methods are and how they work.

First, let's talk about the difference between a host object and a native object. Then you can get into how to create your own objects in JavaScript.

© Russ Ferguson 2019
R. Ferguson, *Beginning JavaScript*, https://doi.org/10.1007/978-1-4842-4395-4_4

Host Object or Native Object

This is not a very long section, but it will clarify the difference between a host object and a native object. Since JavaScript is a language that can work in multiple environments, the code itself may have to act differently in different environments. To illustrate, there may be things in the browser like history or location that will not be available on the server. There may also be other environments like mobile devices that have unique capabilities. For the most part, I will discuss how JavaScript works in the browser.

You may run into the term "isomorphic JavaScript." In this case, it's the ability to have JavaScript applications that can run both on the client side (browser) and the server.

Native (sometimes called built-in) objects are objects that are part of the ECMAScript standard. ECMAScript is not a language itself, but a specification of a scripting language. JavaScript is the most popular implementation of this specification. Other implementations include ActionScript. With that understanding, the ECMAScript specification will define objects independent of the environment. Some of these objects include

- Object
- Array
- Promise
- JSON

Host objects are part of the environment that your code runs in. For example, host objects in your browser include

- Window
- Document
- History
- Navigator

Note If you are interested in what native objects are available to you in the browser, look at the MDN web docs at `https://developer.mozilla.org/en-US/docs/Web/JavaScript/Reference/Global_Objects`.

Many applications you build will take advantage of both types of objects. You will often need one type of object to help work with another.

One of the most-used host objects is the document object. You can use it to inspect what is happening in the current document. An example of this is updating a date for a trip. Using both the document and Date objects, you can update the information in the browser on demand.

Now that you have a good understanding of native objects vs. built-in objects, let's get into some of the details of how to work with a generic object.

Interview Question   What are the differences between host objects and native objects? Name a few.

Explaining Objects

I mentioned being able to group data together. Here I'll start to explain what that means.

In JavaScript, almost everything is an object. An object represents a "thing." Using the concept of things (or nouns) is similar to how you would describe objects in real life. Objects in real life can sometimes be described as having a height, weight, or color.

With that in mind, when wanting to get the details of an object, these details are called *properties*. JavaScript has a long list of built-in properties and methods for objects. Let's ease into the list by starting with the browser's document object.

Introduction to the Document Object

If you want to know the title of the document that is currently loaded in the browser, you can do it like this:

```
let currentTitle = document.title;
```

Here you are creating a variable, just like in the last chapter, and assigning it the value of the title that is in your current document.

In order for this to make sense, let's start on the right side and work backwards. Here you are taking to the document object. This object is provided by the browser (your host environment).

The document object has a property called `title`. You can use what is called dot notation (using a . between words, as in `document.title`) to ask the "What is your title?" question. Using dots, you separate the main thing you are interested in, and then ask for more detail. In this instance, you are asking for the title of your document. If you want to hold onto that information for later use, you need a place to store it.

This is fine if you want to retrieve information from the browser. However, you may find yourself in a situation where you want to update information that is currently in the browser.

The syntax for this is very similar:

```
document.title = "My New Title";
```

You can see that the code is very similar to your earlier example. In this case, you are setting the value of your property and not getting the value (the terms "getter" and "setter" are used often in programing).

Both native and host objects have the ability to process information using properties and something called *methods*. Methods are functions that allow you to perform some kind of process on specific data. An example of this is if you want to find something in your HTML document based on its CSS class. The document object can help you do so:

```
let myClassElements = document.getElementsByClassName('myCssClass');
```

Similar to the title example, the document object will perform a *function* (remember that word for later) that will look at the entire HTML document and send back every single HTML element that is using this class name.

The only thing that this method needs is an argument (the string in quotes). With that, the function knows what to look for.

Other objects in JavaScript are more specific. In the next example, I will discuss what an array is and how you can use it.

Interview Question   How are methods different than properties? What does it mean to use getters and setters?

Arrays and Stacks

An array is a more specialized object. It has features that the generic object does not have. An array is not just good at holding groups of data; it is also good at keeping that data in order.

One way to visualize how an array works is to think of a stack of plates. Each plate in the stack represents data. When discussing the placement of each item in an array, the term that is used is *element*. If you imagine counting the plates from bottom to top, normally you would start the count at one, and that would make sense. There are some programming languages that start the count at one; however, JavaScript starts the count at zero:

```
let myArray = new Array();
    myArray.push('some data'); //count starts at zero
    myArray.push('some other data') //count is now one

console.log(myArray[0]) // some data
```

This is an example of adding data to an array. Every time you add another plate to the stack, the amount of plates in the stack is increased by one. JavaScript arrays calls this the `length`.

I described an array like a stack of plates. Stacks are also a data structure. Questions about data structures can also end up being something that you run into during interviews.

This next example shows how to create an array and start to add values:

```
//create an array using the new operator
let myArray = new Array();

//create an array using square braces
let myOtherArray = [];
```

Here you have different ways of getting the same result. Each one will assign the same properties and methods that belong to an array, to your variable. This will turn your variable into an array object.

Now that you have your array object, you can use the properties and methods that come with it. This example shows how to add data (plates to your stack):

```
let nameArray = new Array();
    nameArray[0] = 'Hunter';
    nameArray[1] = 'Hayes';
    nameArray[2] = 'Grant';
```

Earlier, I spoke about counting your stack of plates. In this example, you assign an index value to each newly created element; the end result is your array or stack.

This is a good way to make sure that a specific element is assigned a value. One of the possible problems you can run into is the ability to add elements out of order. Here is an example:

```
let nameArray = new Array();
    nameArray[0] = 'Hunter';
    nameArray[2] = 'Grant';
```

While this code is correct, and the browser will not tell you that there is anything wrong with it, if you tried to get an element that has not yet been assigned a value, the browser will return undefined.

Getting the Length of an Array

Other languages require you set a number of elements in your array upon creation of the array. JavaScript does not do this. You can add as many elements as you like.

After adding elements to the array, if you want to get a total count of how many elements you are currently working with, you ask for the length:

```
var numberOfElements = myArray.length;
```

In the previous example, you explicitly called out each element by number before adding data to the array. If you just want to add something to the next open slot, the array object has a method called push. This is also a good way to make sure there are no gaps in the number order of your elements.

```
let nameArray = [];
    nameArray.push("Norah");
    nameArray.push("Emily");

let numOfNames = nameArray.length; //return 2
```

With this example, you use the push method to add two names to the array and then you ask for the length of the array. If you want to access each element individually, you ask for each element by its number:

```
console.log(nameArray[0]); //returns Norah
console.log(nameArray[1]); //returns Emily
```

You ask for information about your two elements. Remembering the way JavaScript orders items, you ask for indexes zero and one, and *not* one and two.

You assign strings for the values of your arrays, but it is important to note that an array can hold onto any type of data you like. The purpose of an array is to hold onto groups of data.

Now that you can add information to an array, there are a lot of useful tools built into an array object that you can use. Let's first go over the loops.

Using Loops and Filters

Now that you have information inside your array, you will often find situations where you need to look for a specific value inside that array. You may look for an email address or even if a value is empty. One way of going through all that information is to use a loop. Since this is something that happens often, JavaScript has features built into the array object to let you do that.

```
let myArray = ['one', 'two', 'three', 'four'];
myArray.forEach((value, index, array) => {
    console.log(value); //current value
    console.log(index); //current index
    console.log(array); //entire array
});
```

You learned that objects have both properties and methods. The properties help describe things about the object, and the methods are functions that the object uses to process data.

The array object has a method called forEach. It lets you iterate or go over each element that is in the array.

The way that each item is reviewed is by using a function. I will go over functions in detail in the next chapter. For now, functions are a way of getting the environment to do work for you. When you want some kind of action to take place, you create a function and tell the environment what you need it to do.

In this example, you have the forEach method. Inside this method you add a function. This function is made up of a set of parentheses, an arrow, and some curly braces.

The arrow function is really an equal sign with a greater-than symbol next to it: =>.

The parentheses contain values defining the data that the function has available to it. The values here are placeholders and you can call them whatever you like. To make this clear, I called these parameters value, index, and array (value is the current value of the element that you are looping through, index is the current index number, and array is the entire array).

This example shows a command called console.log. This is something you will see developers use often.

When using the browser developer tools, you will see a section called the console. Here you can output the current value of something that you are working with.

You can also write JavaScript directly in the console. When you hit the return key, it will be executed and will update the current page.

Using the forEach method, you can loop though the entire array. What if you want to filter out some of the information that is inside that array? You can use the filter method to do so. The filter method will return a new array based on the results of the test you create.

To make this work, I will introduce the concept of *conditionals*. Conditionals ask the question "Is this true?"

As you go through the array and use your condition on each value, the result will be a new array:

```
let numberArray = [1,2,3,4,5,6,7,8,9];
let oddNumbers = numberArray.filter((value, index, array) => {
    if(value % 2){
        console.log(value);
        return value;
    }
});
```

Let's break this down in order to understand it better. The array is simply a set of numbers from 1 to 9. The next line is a variable that holds onto the results of the `filter` method. This is similar to what you did before. The method `filter` has a function inside of it. This function has the same properties as the `forEach` method.

What is different is that you are adding a conditional: if the current value is not divisible by 2. If that is a true statement, then take the current value and create a brand-new array from it, and with every other element that falls under the same parameters, add to that new array.

Two other methods built into an array are the `map` and `reduce` methods.

The `map` method lets you loop though all the elements of the array and perform some type of action on each element. A new array is then formed by returning the results of the function, similar to the filter example:

```
let mappedValue = [1,2,3].map( (value, currentValue, currentIndex, array)=>
{
    return value * 10;
});
console.log(mappedValue) //returns [10,20,30]
```

Using the `reduce` method allows you to create a single value by adding all values of the array, using the first value as a starting point, and adding the value of every other element to the first one:

```
let reducedValue = [10,1,2,3,4,5,6,7,8,9].reduce( (value, index, array)=> {
    return value + currentValue;
});
console.log(reducedValue) //returns 55
```

Interview Questions   Given an array of numbers, how do you remove all duplicates and return only unique values? Given the length of an array, what number represents the highest index in that array?

Summary

This chapter covered the concept of objects. In addition, I talked about how there are objects that are native to the language (ECMAScript) and objects exposed to you by the environment (host objects). I also illustrated how objects have both properties and methods. Properties are generality thought of as ways to describe your data, while methods are ways you can act on that data. I used arrays to illustrate this further. Arrays have properties like length, which describes how many elements are inside the array.

Arrays also have methods like push that will add new data to the next available element in the array. This object also has methods or functions that can process the data inside the array, giving you new arrays using the built-in methods.

I introduced conditions, where you can have your program evaluate your data and make choices based on if a certain condition is met. I also introduced arrow functions.

The next chapter will go into more detail about how regular functions work and compare them to arrow functions. I will also discuss the keyword this as well as the concept of context.

CHAPTER 5

JavaScript Functions and Context

The previous chapter introduced the concept of objects and used the array object to illustrate how objects can be used to help you develop your application.

Host objects and environment objects are available to you. Environmental variables may change depending on the environment, so the objects available to you in the browser may not always match what you can use on the server.

This chapter will introduce *functions*. Functions are used as a way to perform options on your data. Functions are also useful because they can be reused as many times as you need.

There are different ways you can create and use functions. You will also learn a few important concepts, such as *context* and *scope*. These concepts will be important in trying to work with other objects and variables. Questions about scope and context come up often in interviews, so it's good to get a solid understanding of how they work. To get started, let's create a simple function.

Making a Function Declaration

This may go by a few names, such as *function declaration, function definition*, or *function statement*. In any case, creating a basic function will require a few things:

- The name of the function

- An optional list of arguments separated by commas

- Code that will perform an operation on the data, surrounded by curly braces

© Russ Ferguson 2019
R. Ferguson, *Beginning JavaScript*, https://doi.org/10.1007/978-1-4842-4395-4_5

This may sound lot more complicated than it really is. Here is some code:

```
function myFunction(optional, data, here ){
      //some code goes here
}
```

This pseudo code example shows a basic function declaration. It starts with the word *function* and then the name you give that function. Inside the parentheses are optional arguments. Depending on what you are doing, the function may need data to work with. Next are the curly braces. Inside the braces you put all the JavaScript code you need for the function to do its job. Let's create a more realistic example:

```
function  addNumbers(num1, num2){
      return num1 + num2;
}

let result = addNumbers(2,3);
console.log(result);
```

This example is simple but more realistic. You have a function with the name addNumbers and two arguments separated by a comma. This is similar to having a variable. They represent numbers that will be used when the function is executed. With that in mind, you perform an operation that adds the two values together and returns a result.

The return command is new, so let's take a moment to explore it. Functions will always return a value and most of the time the value will be undefined. However, if you know you want a value to come back, the return statement is necessary. The return statement will *return* a value to where the function is called.

This example combines a few things from previous chapters. You use the let statement to create a variable called result. The value of this variable will be the result of the function addNumbers.

This is frequently described as *calling* or *executing* a function. You call a function by name and, depending on how the function works, you pass parameters to it.

The last line in this example will output the value in your variable in the browser's console.

In the previous chapter, I explained that almost everything in JavaScript is an object. Since you know that you can assign an object to a variable, you can also do that to a function:

```
const addNumbers = function(num1, num2){ return num1+ num2 };
addNumbers(2,3);
```

Here you create a constant variable and assign your function to it. Then you use the variable in the same way that you would call a function. In this case, the function does not have a name, making it an anonymous function. This is called a *function expression*.

The same thing can be done with named functions. Using a named function helps the debugging process in the case of an error. It makes it easier to find where the error happened.

When reviewing code you will often find a fair amount of function expressions and declarations. However, there are other ways to create functinons with a shorter syntax. This shorter syntax changes the function's relationship to the rest of the code and provides a good introduction to the keyword this and the concept of scope.

Using Arrow Functions

An arrow function expression is a shorter way of creating a function expression. In this section, I will explain some of the differences and introduce the concept of scope and the use of the keyword this.

You will start with a simple arrow function:

```
const arrowFun = (num1, num2)  => { num1 + num2 };
```

Here you create a constant variable just as before. You lose the function keyword and use what is sometimes called a *fat arrow*: =>. The curly braces remain.

You may also notice that you dropped the return keyword. When using an arrow function, if the body of your function is only one line, JavaScript will use what is called an *implicit return*.

This is just one of the ways in which arrow functions are different than the types of functions you used before. Here are some other examples to keep in mind when working with arrow functions:

```
const arrowFun = num1 => num1 * 2;
```

If there is only one argument, you do not need to put it in parentheses.

```
const arrowFun = _ => 2
const arrowFun = () => 2
```

These two statements are the same. If you do not have any arguments to pass over, you can have an empty set of parentheses or use an underscore. Using an underscore is just one less character to type but may be confusing to other developers who are not familiar with all the variations of the arrow function.

```
const arrowFun = (num1, num2) => 2
```

Just like the introductory example, if your function needs more than one argument, then it needs to be in parentheses:

```
const arrowFun = (num1, num2)_ => { if (num1 > num2){
        return 'first is larger than second';
}};
```

If your function's code block (the part between the curly brackets) is more than one line, it then needs a return statement:

```
const arrowFun = () => ({firstName:Paul});
```

Normally, when using functions the code block goes between curly backets. This causes a problem when trying to return an object literal using an arrow function. The reason for this is that the interpreter does not know that you are trying to return an object. The way to fix this is to use parentheses on the outside and create the object literal on the inside.

If you just want a function to do some work for you, either way will do. What makes this one different is the keyword this. Now is a good time to introduce the concept of context and scope with functions.

How Does the Keyword this Work?

I'll first explain what the keyword this is and when you use it. It is not something you declare like a variable or a function. It's more of a starting point.

To illustrate, you are going to create a JavaScript file and look at the value of this from inside an empty JavaScript file. Create an HTML page and use it to load a JavaScript file. Your code should look like Listing 5-1.

Listing 5-1. Load a Simple JavaScript File into the Browser

```
console.log(this)
```

Open the console in the browser developer tools and you should have output that looks like this:

```
Window {postMessage: ƒ, blur: ƒ, focus: ƒ, close: ƒ, frames: Window, ...}
```

I described the keyword this as a starting point. So, in this current instance, this refers to the window object.

In the browser, the window object would be considered a global object. This is not the case if you are working with Node.js. According to the MDN web docs, "a global object is an object that always exists in the global scope." This scope is visible to all other scopes.

In Listing 5-2, you ask for the value of this inside a function. Depending on where the function call is *executed*, it may yield the same results.

Listing 5-2. Get the Current Context of a Function in the Global Scope

```
function getThis()(
    console.log(this)
}

getThis(); //returns Window {postMessage: ƒ, blur: ƒ, focus: ƒ, close: ƒ,
frames: Window, ...}
```

The place in your code where you call a function is called the *execution context*. The execution context determines the value of this.

Note   If you run this code in *strict mode*, the result will be undefined.

The execution context is different when trying to get the value of this from inside an object. See Listing 5-3.

Listing 5-3. Get the Value from Inside an Object

```
var myObj = {
    getThis : function ()(
      console.log(this)
        }
    }
```

```
myObj.getThis() //returns {getThis: f}
```

In this example, the starting point is inside the object myObj. When the method is called, the value of this is the object itself.

Listing 5-4 introduces something new to help explain that the keyword this is tied to the execution context. It will introduce what is called an *IIFE* (immediately invoked function expression). As the name suggests, it is a function that will execute immediately.

Listing 5-4. Referencing a Variable from Inside and Outside the Function Scope

```
(function () {
  var person = "Friend";
  console.log(this); // returns Window {postMessage: f, blur: f, focus: f,
  close: f, frames: Window, ...}
    console.log("Hello " + this,.person); //returns undefined

 console.log("Hello " + person); //returns Hello Friend
})()
```

```
console.log("Hello = " person)_; //returns reference error variable not
defined.
```

Without the need to call the function, this function will execute as soon as it is loaded into the browser.

In the earlier examples, variables declared in the global scope are accessible inside a function. In the current example, the immediately invoked function has its own function scope.

You can see from the output that the function is living inside the global scope. All variables declared inside of the function live inside that function scope.

One of the benefits to this is that variables that would otherwise end up in the global scope will now be in the scope of the IIFE. This is a technique used by many developers to not "pollute" the global scope. Functions and variables will never be part of the global scope. This also prevents overriding other functions or variables that may have the same name.

Interview Question   What is IIFE and how does it prevent functions and variables from polluting the global scope?

The execution context is global but the variable itself is local to the function and not accessible to the last line in the example.

Note that the keyword this is referencing the window object. Trying to use the keyword this to access the variable person will result in a value of undefined being returned.

You can see that referencing properties and methods (variables and functions) using the keyword this can produce unexpected results if you are not careful. JavaScript does provide a few ways to have a more predictable way of controlling the execution context.

Using the call, apply, and bind Methods

When calling a function, the location of where the call happens will determine the execution context of that function. This is one of the reasons why the value of the keyword this varies. Using the bind, apply, or call methods lets you control the context and gives you a more predictable way of using this.

Let's start with the bind keyword. You can set the object that the keyword this will use as a starting point. Listing 5-5 shows an example.

Listing 5-5. Using the Keyword bind to Set the Value of this

```
var myObj = {
    person: "Friend"
}

function sayHello() {
     console.log("Hello " + this.person);
}
```

```
sayHello() //returns Hello undefined
```

```
var tryAgain = sayHello.bind(myObj) //assigning the value of this to the
object myObj
```

```
tryAgain() // returns Hello Friend
```

Using bind, you set the object that you want to use as a starting point. In this example, you set the value to the object called myObj.

With myObj as a starting point, you can then access properties of the object (in this case the person property) without running into an error where the browser declares the value undefined.

The call and apply methods are similar. The main difference is, not only can you define the execution context, but you can also pass information to the method that you want to execute. Listing 5-6 shows an example of calling the call method.

Listing 5-6. Using the call Method

```
sayHello(message){
  console.log(message, this.mainCharacter);
}

const  characters = {
      mainCharacter: "Elliot"
}

sayHello.call(characters, "Hello "); //returns Hello Elliot
```

Functions in JavaScript are objects. These function objects have their own set of properties and methods associated with them.

In Listing 5-7, you use the call method to dictate the execution context of the function you want to work with. You tell the function sayHello to use the call method and assign both the starting point of execution context to the characters object and also pass a list of parameters to the sayHello function where it can execute properly. In this example, you only pass one.

The apply method is very similar. The big difference is that the apply method expects an array.

Listing 5-7. Using the call Method

```
sayHello(firstName, secondName, thirdName){
  console.log(this.message, firstName); //returns Hello Elliot
  console.log(this.message, secondName); //returns Hello Tyrell
  console.log(this.message, thirdName); //returns Hello Dominique
}

const show = {
      message: "Hello"
}

sayHello.apply(show, ["Elliot ", " Tyrell ", "Dominique ");
```

Interview Questions   What is the execution context of a function and can you change it? What object can be found in the global scope in the browser?

Here your function is similar to what you did with the `call` method. Passing an array lets you use elements of that array as parameters of a function.

You can see from these examples that using the keyword `this` can take on many different forms depending on how it is used.

It is also important to remember that a function is also an object (native or host object) and these objects have their own properties and methods. The methods you learned were `call`, `apply`, and `bind`. These methods help control the execution context, which controls the value of the keyword `this`.

Something that you will find as you work with other developers is *closures*. A simple explanation is that a closure is a function inside a function. In the next section, you will explore how closures work.

Understanding Closures

In the last section, I explained the idea of a closure as a function inside another function. Because of the way JavaScript handles scope when using functions, you can do some interesting things.

Functions and variables that are created *inside* a function live in what is called the *lexical scope*. The inner function has access to the variables and functions not just in its own scope but in both the outer function scope and the global scope. It is also important to note that this does not work in the other direction.

Listing 5-8 shows how the inner function can access variables outside of itself.

Listing 5-8. Using a Closure to Illustrate an Inner Function's Access to Other Scopes

```
sayHello(firstName, lastName){
  let msg = "Greetings ";
    function intro(){
      return  msg + firstName = " " + lastName;
    }

 return into();

}

sayHello("Professor" , "Falken");  //returns "Greetings Professor Falken";
```

This example illustrates how the inner function has access to the outer function. The outer function executes the inner function (`intro`) and returns the results to where it was called. The inner function returns a string that is made up of variables from both the outer function and the inner function. The results then display in the browser console using the `console.log` method.

If you came from other languages like Java, you should be familiar with the idea of declaring public and private methods and properties. These languages allow you to hide some of the inner workings of how a method processes information inside a class when a public method is called.

JavaScript does not provide that ability, but by using a closure you can write code that has the same effect. Listing 5-9 shows an example of where a variable is not immediately accessible without using a function to access it.

Listing 5-9. Using a Closure to Create Private Variables

```
const sayHello = function(){
      let greetingMsg = "Greetings ";

      function msgTo(firstName, lastName){
         greetingMsg = greetingMsg + firstName + " " + lastName;
      }

   return {
            sendGreeting: function(firstName, lastName){
                  msgTo(firstName, lastName);
            }

            getMsg: function(){
                  return greetingMsg;
            }
      }
  }

const createMsg = sayHello();
createMsg.sendGreeting(("Professor" , "Falken");
console.log(creatMsg.getMsg()); //returns "Greetings Professor Falken";
```

In this example, you declare a closure and assign it to the variable sayHello. The closure, when called, returns an object whose methods have access to a variable that is outside their function scope.

Calling the function sayHello returns an object with two methods, sendGreeting and getMsg.

Calling the sendGreeting method updates the variable greetingMsg. This variable is not accessible any way other than using the sendGreeting function.

To see the updated variable, you call the other method, getMsg. It looks at the internal variable and returns its updated value. In this case, you get the message "Greetings Professor Falken."

Because the variable greetingMsg is inside the outer function, it is not accessible from the global scope.

It is also important to note that if you assign the result of sayHello to a second variable, it will be independent of the first instance. The way the functions execute will be exactly the same. However, the values may be different. Here is an example:

```
const createMgs2 = sayHello();
createMsg2.sendGreeting("David", "Lightman");
console.log (createMsg2.getMg()); //returns Greetings David Lightman
```

Here you are use the exact same functions and end up with different results.

Interview Question   How do you create private variables in JavaScript?

Summary

This chapter started to outline how functions are important for application development. You explored topics like how to control the execution context of a function using methods like call, apply, and bind. You also went over how the keyword this has different meanings depending on the execution context.

This chapter also discussed the differences between function expressions and arrow functions and why understanding what makes them different is important.

Closures and IIFEs were also discussed. Immediately invoked functions are a way of keeping variables and methods out of the global scope, while closures are a way to create private variables and methods similar to what someone coming from a strongly typed language like Java would understand.

Functions are an important part of JavaScript. What is also important is the ability to call a function. Often functions are called as a result of an event. The next chapter will cover how events work in JavaScript. It will also cover events that come from the environment and events that the user creates.

CHAPTER 6

JavaScript and Events

In the last chapter, you learned how functions work and the difference between arrow functions and function expressions. You also learned how the execution context controls the keyword this and the built-in methods used to create a more predicable way of working with it.

Functions are often called because of an *event*. Events can be things like a page loading or a button click. JavaScript allows you to "listen" for events and then execute a function in response to the event.

In this chapter, you will learn how to use the combined knowledge from the previous chapters and start to develop some interaction with the browser using events. You will also explore the concept of *event bubbling*.

There may also be times where the built-in events do not cover what you want to do. You can then make custom events for your application.

The document object is one of many objects that include a method called addEventListener. This method takes two arguments, the event that you are listening for and a function that will do something when the event happens.

There is a long list of events for the environment (https://developer.mozilla.org/en-US/docs/Web/Events) that you are working with, but for this example let's just figure out when the page is loaded.

In this example, you are going to listen for the event DOMContentLoaded. The event DOMContentLoaded lets you know that the content of the page has loaded into the browser and has been parsed. Listing 6-1 shows an example of this in action.

Listing 6-1. Adding an Event Listener to Know When the Page Loaded

```
document.addEventListener("DOMContentLoaded", function(){
    console.log(this); //returns #document
});
```

© Russ Ferguson 2019
R. Ferguson, *Beginning JavaScript*, https://doi.org/10.1007/978-1-4842-4395-4_6

When you open the console in the browser developer tools, you will see the result of this event. It should give you access to the entire document that just loaded. At the moment, there is not much in the document, but the takeaway is that this anonymous function was executed when the event occurred.

Interview Question   Name an event that lets you know that the contents of the page have been both loaded and parsed.

Event listeners can be added and removed. This gives you flexibility when you want to assign a different listener to the same object.

Listing 6-2 shows an example of both adding and removing an event listener to a button.

Listing 6-2. Adding and Removing Event Listeners

```
document.addEventListener("DOMContentLoaded",onPageLoad);

function onPageLoad(){
    let theButton = document.getElementById("myButton");
        theButton.addEventListener("click", handleButtonClick);
}

function handleButtonclick(){
    console.log("button clicked");
    let theButton = document.getElementById("myButton");
        theButton.removeEventListener("click", handleButtonClick);
}
```

This example uses a named function instead of an anonymous function. The logic goes like this. The event DOMContentLoaded gets fired and calls the function onPageLoad. This function creates a local variable called theButton and references the button in the HTML page by its id. It then adds an event listener, waiting for the button to be clicked.

When the button is clicked, it calls a function named handelButtonClick. This function prints out in the console that the button was clicked. Then it creates its own local variable that references the same button in the document and removes the event listener. This make the button inactive when the user wants to click on it a second time.

Here you are using the `DOMContentLoaded` event to set up the application to do everything you want.

When the page loads, you add the event listener to the button. In this use case, you only want it to be active for one click. When the button is clicked, you remove the event listener, making it inactive using named functions. This is helpful because in the case of an error, you can reference the functions directly, which you can't do if you are using anonymous functions.

Adding event listeners to objects also lets you add listeners for different types of events. Listing 6-3 shows an example where you add multiple events to the same button.

Listing 6-3. Adding Multiple Events to a Button

```
document.addEventListener("DOMContentLoaded",onPageLoad);

function onPageLoad(){
    let theButton = document.getElementById("myButton");
        theButton.addEventListener("click", handleButtonClick);
        theButton.addEventListener("mouseover", mouseOverEvent);
        theButton.addEventListener("mouseout", mouseOutEvent);
}

function handleButtonclick(){
    console.log("button clicked");
}

function mouseOverEvent (){
    console.log("mouseover");
}

function mouseOutEvent (){
    console.log("mouseout");
}
```

You use the `DOMContentLoaded` event to tell the application to add multiple event listeners to your button. These listeners know when the button is clicked, rolled over, and rolled off. In each instance, when the event is triggered, it fires off a function that prints out a message in the browser console.

There may be times when you want to stop the browser from doing something it would normally do and have JavaScript take over. The next section will address this using the preventDeault method.

Using preventDefault

Some examples of preventing the browser from performing its normal functions are when using links or forms. Links are usually thought of as a way to go to another page in the site.

If you want to have someone click a link, and not have the browser go to another page, you can use the preventDefault method.

The event object gets passed to the event handler function when an event happens. This object contains information about the event that just happened.

For example, if you want to know about the link that was clicked, you can ask for the target. Listing 6-4 shows an example.

Listing 6-4. Finding the Object That Was Clicked

```
document.addEventListener("DOMContentLoaded",onPageLoad);


function onPageLoad(){
let  theButton = document.getElementById("myLink");
     theButton. addEventListener("click", function(evt){
      evt.preventDefault();
      console.log(evt);
      console.log(evt.target);
});
```

This example is similar to the previous examples where when the document is loaded the click event listener is added to an anchor tag inside the HTML page by its id.

Once clicked, an event object is passed to the function containing information about the event that just occurred. One of the methods that this object possesses is the preventDefault method. It keeps the browser from going to the URL assigned to the link.

You can also see the entire event object by using the console.log method. It prints the results in the browser developer tools.

The next line displays the target. This is the object that dispatched the event. In your case, it's the item that was clicked. The developer tools show the HTML of the target.

Forms usually go to another page on submission. If you run into a situation where you want to do something like validation on the contents of the form before submission, you can prevent the form from summiting the content to the server. This will give you an opportunity to validate the form before sending the data.

When using JavaScript to prevent the browser from submitting the form until after the contents have been validated, you can also use the preventDefault method. See Listing 6-5.

Listing 6-5. Using the preventDefault Method with a Form

```
document.addEventListener("DOMContentLoaded",onPageLoad);

function onPageLoad(){
    let myForm = document.querySelector("form");
        myForm.addEventListener("submit", onSubmit);
}

function onSubmit(evt){
   console.log("form submitted");
  evt.,preventDefault();
}
```

Using some of code from other examples, you wait for the DOMContentLoaded event to happen. Once that event happens, you call the onPageLoad function.

The querySelector method searches for the form object that is in the HTML page. You then add an event listener to the form, wanting to know when it will try to submit any data.

When the submit button is clicked, the submit event triggers the onSubmit function. This overrides the browser trying to submit the data and go to another HTML page by using the preventDefault method.

It also prints the message "form submitted" in the console. Using this method will make sure that the browser does not do anything unexpected.

Interview Question   How do you stop the browser from performing its normal functions?

You have seen instances where you can control how a browser normally works. This gives you an opportunity to do things like evaluate the data before submission or create a single page application where you do not need to go to another HTML page.

A large amount of work in the browser is tied to events. An important concept to understand is that of *event propagation*. Event propagation is when you want to discuss both the bubbling phase and the capture phase of an event. The next section will explain this in detail.

Event Propagation

Event propagation deals with how various objects in the browser are able to receive events. In the last section, I showed how you can assign a listener to an object. That object will wait for an event to happen and then call a function to handle the event.

One phase of propagation is *event bubbling*. An example of this is when a button inside a `div` is clicked. The `target` of the click is the button itself.

However, the event travels up from the button to its parent. This process will continue until the event meets the `window` object. Listing 6-6 shows how this works.

Listing 6-6. Illustrating Event Bubbling

```
document.addEventListener("DOMContentLoaded",onPageLoad);

function onPageLoad(){
  let myButton = document.getElementById("myButton");
      myButton.addEventListener("click", onButtonClick);

  let container = document.getElelmentById("container");
      container.addEventeListener("click", onContainerClick);

    document.addEventListener("click", onDocumentClick);
    window.addEventListener("click", onWindowClick);

}
```

```
function onButtonClick (evt){
    console.log("button clicked");
}

function onContainerClick (evt){
    console.log("container clicked");
}
function onDocumentClick (evt){
    console.log("document clicked");
}

function onWindowClick (evt){
    console.log("window clicked");
}
```

A pattern is emerging: you wait for the document to load and then you assign event listeners to items in the HTML document.

In this case, you are looking for the button with the ID of myButton. When the listener is added, it calls the function onButtonClick and prints out in the console that the button was clicked.

Because of event bubbling, the event then goes up to the div tag and its event listener handles the event.

Moving on from there, both the document and the window objects can handle the event. You can see the results in the browser console:

```
button click
container click
documnnt click
window click
```

You can see that once the button has been clicked, the event travels up to the window object without you needing to do anything. This is the default way that browsers handle events. You can stop this from happening by using the stopPropagation method. It keeps the other objects from listening to events as they bubble up.

Listing 6-7 is mostly the same as Listing 6-6. The only difference is the addition of the stopPropagation method after the div tag receives the event. This keeps the document and the window from receiving the event.

Listing 6-7. Using the stopPropagation Method

```
function onContainerClick(evt){
  console.log("container clicked");
  evt.stopPropagation();
}
```

This is not a full example of the code; I just show the important parts to illustrate the example. When an event is called, the event object is sent to an event handler. You use this object to call the stopPropagation method.

This prevents any of the other objects higher up in the chain from receiving the event, even if they have listeners for that event.

Another way that browsers can work with events is though *event capturing*. This is the exact opposite of what you have been doing with bubbling, where the browser starts at the top of the document and works its way down to the target.

To have the browser use this method of dealing with events, you need to tell the addEventListener method to use capturing and not bubbling. Listing 6-8 shows how the event travels down from the window object.

Listing 6-8. Using Event Capturing

```
function onPageLoad(){
   let myButton = document.getElementById("myButton");
       myButton.addEventListener("click", onButtonClick, true);

 let container = document.getElementById("container");
     container.addEventListener("click", onContainerClick, true);

     document.addEventListener("click", onDocumentClick, true);
   window.addEventListener("click", onWinowClick, true);
'}
```

Adding the last property to the addEventListener method tells the browser to enable *event capturing*. The stack then starts from the top down:

```
window click
documnnt click
container click
button click
```

Adding the last property to the addEventListener method tells the browser to enable *event capturing*. The stack then starts from the top down.

These two examples showed how events can move though the browser, either from the source of the event to the top or from the window object down.

At this point, the events you used have been built into the environment. There may be times when you need to make a custom event. The next section will cover how to make that happen.

Interview Questions   What is the difference between event bubbling and capturing? How can you prevent them from happening?

Creating Custom Events

Most of the time, when you need to know when something is happening in your application, you can use an event that is already built into the environment. However, there may be a situation where the built-in events may not always line up with your needs. This is where custom events come in.

Most of what you have worked with is exactly the same. You need to listen for an event, and that event needs to be dispatched. One of the differences here is that you will dispatch your own custom event. Listing 6-9 is an example of a custom event.

Listing 6-9. Creating and Using Custom Events

```
function onPageLoad(){
   let myButton = document.getElementById("myButton");
      myButton.addEventListener("click", onButtonClick, true);
      myButton.addEventLIstener("WORLD_ENDING_EVENT", onWorldEnd);

}

function onButtonClick(evt){
   let custEvent = new CustomEvent("WORLD_ENDING_EVENT", {
    detail: message: { "And I feel fine"}
    });
```

```
    let myButton = document.getElementById("myButton");
        myButton.dispatchEvent(custEvent);
};

functon onWorldEnd(evt){
    console.log(evt); // returns  CustomEvent {isTrusted: false, detail:
    {...}, type: "WORLD_ENDING_EVENT", target: button#myButton,
    currentTarget: button#myButton, ...}
    console.log(evt.type); //returns WORLD_ENDING_EVENT
    console.log(evt.detail); //returns {message: "And I feel fine"}
}
```

The button is listening for two different types of events. The first is the normal click event, and the other is the custom WORLD_ENDING_EVENT. Since it's not on the list of events that either the environment or the JavaScript language provides, it must be a custom event.

The code for listening for this event is the same as for any other event. You add the name and then the event handler function that will execute when the event happens.

In this case, the function is called onWorldEnd and it prints out the different values of the event object that is sent over to the function. The first example prints out the entire event object. The second prints out the type property of the event object. The last one prints out the value of the detail object that is sent from the custom event.

Interview Question   How do you implement custom events?

Summary

Events are a vital part of application development. Events can give you an idea of what is happening in the environment as well as what you user is doing.

This chapter covered what events are, some of the events that are part of the environment, and how to make your own custom events. You now know how to listen for events, and that there is no difference between custom events and native events.

Event handlers can use both anonymous functions and named functions. Event objects are passed to function handlers to describe everything about the function that just happened. Using an event object, you can see what HTML element dispatched the event, and you have the ability to stop the browser from performing some of its native operations. You also have a clearer understanding of how events propagate though the browser and how to control them.

The next chapter will go over the idea of inheritance in JavaScript. You will learn how to create a class and the difference between composition and inheritance.

CHAPTER 7

JavaScript and Programming Paradigms

In this chapter, I will explain some of the different programming paradigms you can use with JavaScript. By programming paradigms I mean the different ways or "styles" in which you can write your JavaScript code.

JavaScript is a flexible language. This chapter will cover two main programming paradigms: object-oriented programming (OOP) and functional programing. In an interview, you may be asked to explain the difference between the two paradigms. In addition, you may find code written by other developers that may fall into one or both of these categories.

Interview Question   Name two different programming paradigms used with JavaScript.

Object-Oriented Programming with JavaScript

Objects can be thought of as things that can do work for you. Arrays can hold onto a group (or stack) of data. The `Math` object can perform calculations for you. Inside any environment that can run JavaScript is a long list of objects that you can use.

Object-oriented programming is a paradigm where you can both create your own objects that will perform specific actions for you and use the objects that are available in the environment.

When talking about objects in this way, they are often compared to things in real life. Tutorials often use people as an example to explain how an object works. You can have a group of people in a room. They share similar traits, such as height, hair color, and first and last names.

© Russ Ferguson 2019
R. Ferguson, *Beginning JavaScript*, https://doi.org/10.1007/978-1-4842-4395-4_7

Even with all of these similarities, they are still individuals. This gives you the opportunity to group the things that you know are similar and abstract them into what is called a *class.*

A class is often thought of as a blueprint. Inside this blueprint is code that deals with all the things you know about a person, without any of the details.

In the next example, you will use the ES6 `class` keyword. There are other ways to do this but for the sake of clarity you are going to use the most current syntax. Once you get used to this, you will learn other ways to create classes in JavaScript.

If you want to add details to your object, you can create an *instance* of this class. An instance is an object that instantiated from the class. This instance has all the methods and properties that were defined inside the class. If a class is the blueprint, the instance can be thought of as the thing that is built from that blueprint.

Before you go too far, you should see this in code, so please look at Listing 7-1.

Listing 7-1. Creating a Robot Class

```
7-1.js
class Robot {
    constructor(name, type){
        this.name = name;
        this.type = type;
        this.greeting = function(){
        return "I'm " + this.name + " I'm a " + this.type + ".";
        }
    }
}
```

Create a HTML page that points to a JavaScript file with this code in it. Load the HTML page in your browser. This will load the class into the browser's memory. Now you can create instances using the browser console. With the developer tools open, you can execute the code that was loaded from the JavaScript page.

In this example, you are creating an object based on the Robot class. To create an instance, you first make a variable and then assign it the value of a new instance of the Robot class.

When creating the instance, you pass over two arguments for the class to use. Just like when passing data to a function, this class will consume the arguments and use them internally.

You can see the results by calling the method `greeting` that is part of the class. Figure 7-1 shows an example of creating two instances based on the same class.

In Figure 7-1, you can see two different instances of the same Robot class. Each instance holds on to its own data.

```
> let bender = new Robot("Bender", "Bending Robot");
< undefined
> bender.greeting();
< "My name is Bender I'm a Bending Robot."
> let r2d2 = new Robot("R2D2", "Astromech Droid");
< undefined
> r2d2.greeting();
< "My name is R2D2 I'm a Astromech Droid."
> |
```

Figure 7-1. *Creating two instances of the Robot class*

Looking at the Robot class, you can refer to the chapter about objects. Using the keyword this lets you keep the values of the properties name and type inside the object.

You may notice that the class starts with a capital letter. This is a convention for creating classes with JavaScript.

When creating a class instance, you use the keyword new. This creates an object that contains all the properties and methods defined in that class. Depending on how the class has been defined, each instance can have unique values. This gives you the ability to instantiate or create multiple instances of the class, each holding different properties.

The constructor function inside your class takes the properties that were passed when you created an instance and assigns them to the instance.

At this point, you have abstracted out some of the more generic properties of your robot. There may be a time when you want to combine the generic properties with some that are more specific to the robot in question.

Children of the Atom

In the last section, you abstracted some generic properties of a robot and were able to use that blueprint as a way to instantiate individual instances of the Robot class. Now let's have these robots perform some specific tasks based on their type. This means that you need to make *child* classes that will *inherit* properties from a *parent* class. Listing 7-2 explores the concept of extending the parent class.

Listing 7-2. Inheriating from a Parent Class Using the ES6 extends Keyword

```
7-2.js
class BendingUnit extends Robot {
    constructor(name, type){
        super(name, type);
        }
    }
}
```

This code uses the extends keyword to tell the environment that it wants to use everything that is available from the *parent* class Robot in addition to the features in this current class.

Since you know that you want to use some of the properties and methods of the *parent* class, you use the keyword super to pass over everything the parent class needs to function property, in your case the same two properties.

At this moment, you are not adding anything new to the BendingUnit class, but if you create an object from this class and run the same methods from the parent class, you will get the same results.

Creating this object is the same as in the last example. There is nothing special you need to do just because this is a child of a parent object. The class's internal functions will take care of that part. Figure 7-2 should look very similar at this point.

```
> let bendingUnit = new BendingUnit("Bender", "Benging Unit");
< undefined
> bendingUnit.greeting();
< "My name is Bender I'm a Benging Unit."
>
```

Figure 7-2. *Creating a class that extends functions from a parent class*

You can see that even though the name property and the greeting method do not exist in this class, they are available because you are extending from the Robot class. By use of the extends keyword, you inherit these properties and methods.

Now that you have the ability to reuse functions from your parent class, you can also create unique functions for the subclasses. See Listing 7-3.

Listing 7-3. Creating Unique Methods for the Robot Subclass

7-3.js
```
class BendingUnit extends Robot {
   constructor(name, type){
       super(name, type);
       }
     primaryFunction(){
     cosole.log(this.name + " bends things");
     }
   }

let bendingUnit = new BendingUnit("Bender", "Bending Robot");
bendingUnit.primaryFunction(); //returns Bender bends things.
```

In this example, you have a method that is unique to the current class and is not dependent on the parent class. This method still can take advantage of the properties of the parent class to perform its unique features.

Create an object just like in the last example and call it `primaryFunction`. The result should be just like in Listing 7-3.

This is how inheritance works. You can abstract properties and functions into a class, and then for more detail you can create a subclass that can take advantage of the parent while adding its own unique features.

Using the `extends` keyword gives you the ability to inherit from another class. JavaScript only allows you to inherit from one parent class.

Since you are using the ES6 syntax for your class, there is a lot going on behind the scenes. The next section will give you a chance to dive under the covers and explore.

JavaScript Classes and Prototypical Inheritance

In the last section, you used the keyword `extends` to begin your exploration of the topic of inheritance. The idea is that an object can gain the properties and methods of another class. This other class is considered its *super* or *parent class.*

Other languages have what can be described as classed-based inheritance. This means that an object can inherit its properties and methods from other classes.

JavaScript, however, is *prototype based*, meaning that if the property or method does not exist in the current object, it will look at the *prototype* property of the object and move to its parent object to see if the property exists there. This is often called moving up the *prototype chain.*

In the previous examples, you used the ES6 syntax to create objects. One of the keywords you used was `constructor`. A function constructor is really just a function that creates a function object.

To make a proper comparison, let's recreate the `robot` class using a function constructor. See Listing 7-4.

Listing 7-4. Creating the Robot Object Using Function Contructors

```
7-4.js
const Robot = function(name, type) {
    this.name = name;
    this.type = type;
}
```

```
Robot.prototype.greeting = function(){
      return "I'm " + this.name + " I'm a " + this.type + ".";
}

let bender = new Robot ("Bender", "Bending Robot");
bender.greeting() // "My name is Bender I'm a Bending Robot."
```

Here you create a constant and assign a function to it. This function takes two properties and assigns the values to its internal object.

The next line is where you start to get into how inheritance in JavaScript really works. You access the prototype property of your object and create a function called greeting. This is just like creating a function using the class syntax.

Properties and methods are added to the object's prototype. This means if there are any classes that can inherit from this class, JavaScript moves up the *prototype chain* from the child object to its parent objects to access the property.

Listing 7-5 shows how to create an object that will inherit methods and properties from another object.

Listing 7-5. Creating Inheritance Without Using the ES6 Syntax

```
7-5.js
const Robot = function(name, type) {
      this.name = name;
      this.type = type;
    }

Robot.prototype.greeting = function(){
      return "I'm " + this.name + " I'm a " + this.type + ".";
}

const BendingUnit = function(){
    Robot.apply(this, arguments);
}

BendingUnit.prototype = Object.create(Robot.prototype);
BendingUnit.prototype.constructor = BendingUnit;

let bender = new BendingUnit("Bender", "Bending Unit");
bender.greeting() // "My name is Bender I'm a Bending Unit."
```

One of the key differences here is that the function `BendingUnit` is calling the original `Robot` class and using the `apply` method.

The `apply` method tells the browser that the `BendingUnit` class can be used as a starting point to access the properties of the `Robot` class.

The next line tells the environment to update the prototype object of the `BendingUnit` class and assign to it the value of the `Robot` prototype.

Now that the prototype has been updated, the constructor thinks that is a copy of the `Robot` class and not its own `BendingUnit` class.

To fix this, assign the contractor function to the `BendingUnit` function, so it will know that even though it inherits functions from the `Robot` class, it itself is not the *Robot*.

The last two lines in this example function the same way as when you were using the ES6 syntax. You can see that using the ES5 syntax puts you closer to how JavaScript really works but may make explaining the concept of inheritance more difficult.

Overall, inheritance is useful for reusing code without having to rewrite it. There is another pattern called *composition*. Using composition, you create objects inside the class and use them directly without the need for inheritance. This is not a feature of the JavaScript language but a way to reuse code to give objects more ability.

One of the criticisms of inheritance is that not only do you inherit features you want but you can also inherit features that you do not need. This is because they are part of a parent class or a parent's parent class.

In the next section, I will discuss the other paradigm: functional programming with JavaScript.

Functional Programming with JavaScript

As mentioned, JavaScript is a very flexible language. The two paradigms often used are object-oriented programing and functional programing.

Previously you created objects in JavaScript using both the ES6 syntax that contains the keyword `class` and the ES5 syntax that relies on your understanding of prototypical inheritance.

Understanding prototypical inheritance is very important when working with JavaScript. However, functional programing does not rely on prototypes.

Functional programing has a few concepts that need explaining in order to get a full understanding of how it is different from object-oriented programing.

Some of the concepts I will cover are

- Pure functions

- Side effects/shared state

- Immutability

- Declarative over imperative code

Pure Functions

What makes it pure is that no matter how many times you call the function, the result will always be the same. If you have a function that takes a number, multiplies it by two (x * 2), and then returns the result, the results will be consistent no matter what numbers you pass to the function. Listing 7-6 shows an example of a pure function.

Listing 7-6. Creating a Pure Function

```
7-6.js
const timesTwo = (x) =>  x * 2;

timesTwo(2) //returns 4
timesTwo(3) //returns 6
```

This gives your function something called *referential transparency*. This means that you can virtually replace the function itself with the value it returns and the behavior of the application will not change. If this is not the case, it is called *referentially opaque*.

What makes a function impure is if the function returns different results despite passing the same values into it. For example, developers sometimes want to make a call to a service that has unique properties every time to prevent the browser from caching the results. To do this, they add the current time into the URL. Because you can only get the exact time right once in a 24-hour period, this is not a pure function. Anything that makes the function produce inconsistent results or has to do anything in addition to returning a value will make the function impure.

Side Effects/Shared State

Another feature of pure functions is that they do not produce *side effects*, meaning that they do not change or *mutate* objects that are accessible outside the function.

Because JavaScript passes object properties as a *reference*, when a change is made to the property of the object or array, it mutates the state of that object. That same object can be accessible outside of the function. Pure functions must not change the external state.

Tip   JavaScript variables that are assigned to a non-primitive value (an object) are given a reference to that value. The reference refers to the object's location in the computer's memory. The variable itself does not contain the value.

Immutability

Immutability is an important concept of functional programming. The idea that an object is not changed or *mutated* makes somethings like debugging simpler because each state is constant.

As a reminder, using the keyword `const` will keep variables constant but does not prevent objects from being updated.

One thing that often happens is that you have a situation where you would normally mutate the data, an array for example. If you are programing in a functional way, you do not want to mutate the data. How can you resolve this?

In this case, you can make a copy of the data and send the copy back as a result. This keeps you from mutating the original object and gives you the results you need.

To add items to an array, most people would use the `push` method. This adds an item to the end of the array. However, this also mutates the array. To resolve this, you can use the built-in `Object` datatype and use the `assign` method. To make this clearer, look at Listing 7-7.

Listing 7-7. Returning a Copy of an Array So Data Is Not Mutated

```
7-7.js
const twoArray = ["One", "Two"];
const threeArray = Object.assign([...twoArray], {2:"Three"});
console,log(threeArray); //returns (3) ["One", "Two", "Three"]
```

In this example, the first line creates an array. The second line uses the `assign` method. This method receives two arguments. The first is the original array. Instead of looping though the entire array to get all the elements, you use the spread operator to pass over all the properties of an iterable object, in this case the array. The second parameter is the object that you want to add to the array. This will create a new array and not mutate the original object.

Declarative Over Imperative Code

The main difference between declarative vs. imperative code is that imperative code goes through the steps to describe how to achieve the desired result. While declarative code focuses on what should happen to the data, the details of how it should work are abstracted away. Listing 7-8 shows an example where you make a new array based on an existing one.

Listing 7-8. Imperative Code vs. Declarative Code

```
7-8.js
const threeArray = ["One", "Two", "Three"];
//Imperative code describing how a program operates
for(let i = 0; threeArray.length > i; i++){
    console.log(threeArray[i]); //returns One, Two, Three
}

//Declarative code showing how a program should work
 threeArray.map((value, index, arr) => {
    console.log(value); //returns One, Two, Three
});
```

The first instance shows a way to loop though the data based on the length of the array. There are checks in the `for` loop to figure out how far you can go.

The second instance takes advantage of the built-in `map` method. This method takes a function as an argument. The function receives each item in the array without needing to know the length of the array.

The major difference here is that you do not need to describe how you navigate through the data. The focus is only on what you do with the data.

These are important concepts to understand if you are working in a functional programming environment. Functions in JavaScript can be passed as properties of a function. They can also be values returned from other functions.

The ability to chain functions is something that you will see often. Using the `fetch` method to retrieve data from a remote source requires chaining the method and *then* processing the results that return from the server. Here is an example:

```
fetch('https://swapi.co/api/people/1').then(results => results.json()).
then(json => console.log(json));

//results
//{name: "Luke Skywalker", height: "172", mass: "77", hair_color: "blond",
skin_color: "fair", ...}
```

Here you use the `fetch` method to retrieve data from the Star Wars API (`https://swapi.co`). This method returns what is called a *promise*. It will wait until the request is resolved or fails.

When the request is resolved, the `then` method is chained to it. Here you can process the results. The first `then` method takes the results and converts them into a JSON object. When using arrow functions, the result is automatically returned when there are no curly braces and only one line of code.

This is sent over to the second `then` method, where the results of the first method become a parameter called `json` and are printed in the browser console.

Summary

In this chapter, you explored two different styles or paradigms of programming. The first was object-oriented programing where you created objects that represented things that you wanted to model.

It is important to remember that JavaScript uses prototypes to create inheritance. Properties and methods that do not exist in the current object move up the prototype chain to the object's parent class.

The second is functional programming, where pure functions become extremely important. These functions always return the same results if the same arguments are passed to the function. They also do not create *side effects* where they do more than just return a consistent value.

You also learned the concept of immutability. Objects are not updated directly; this would mutate the object. Instead, a copy is made and the changes are added to that copy and are sent back to the application.

The last section covered the difference between declarative vs. imperative code. Declarative code uses code to figure out how to navigate thought the data, and imperative code allows the code to figure out on its own how it should present itself and lets you focus on what you want to do with it. The example used the map method of the array; it allowed you to go through each item in the array without knowing the length ahead of time.

The next chapter will cover how to use the tools in your browser to help debug your application. Understanding how these tools work will be very helpful as your applications get more complex.

CHAPTER 8

JavaScript and Debugging

Up to this point, I have discussed how to install software and some of the important things you need to know when working with JavaScript. For the most part, JavaScript is something that you work with in the browser.

That being that case, if the code you wrote works, the results will be displayed in the browser. More importantly, if the results do not work, you need a way to see what went wrong.

The question then becomes, "How can I see what is happening to my code in the browser?" Happily, browsers have debugging tools built in. This chapter will go over some tools you can work with while trying to debug your code in the browser.

Firefox has a browser specifically for developers, Firefox Developer Edition (`www.mozilla.org/en-US/firefox/developer/`) has tools, which are unique to that browser.

At the time of writing, Google's Chrome browser remains the most popular. For that reason, I'll use the development tools in that browser as a reference.

Developer tools are made up of different panels. While I won't go over each panel in detail, there are panels that are specific for certain tasks. Some of these panels include

- Device mode
- Elements panel
- Console panel
- Sources panel
- Network panel
- Performance panel
- Memory panel
- Application panel
- Security panel

© Russ Ferguson 2019
R. Ferguson, *Beginning JavaScript*, https://doi.org/10.1007/978-1-4842-4395-4_8

The Console Panel

In previous chapters, you used the Console panel. This let you execute JavaScript directly in the browser and get results back. You were also able to call functions that were defined in JavaScript files that were loaded into the browser.

Since you have worked with the console in the past, this is a good place to start. To open the browser console, right-click the page and select the Inspect option. This opens the developer tools. If you want to use keyboard commands, select Command + Option + J (on the Mac) or Control + Shift + J (on Windows). See Figure 8-1.

Figure 8-1. *Displaying the Console panel*

The console has its own API (application programming interface). The purpose of the console is to give you insight into the code that you are working with as it is being executed.

So far, you just used the `console.log` method to have the browser print out results for you. This is helpful but it's not the only way you can use the console to help you understand what is happening in the browser.

Some of these functions are self-explanatory. For example, `console.clear()` will clear everything in the console.

The only exception with using the `clear` method is if the *Preserve Log* setting is checked off. This will preserve the history of what you have been working on in the console between page refreshes. You can find it by clicking the cog on the right side of the developer tools window. See Figure 8-2.

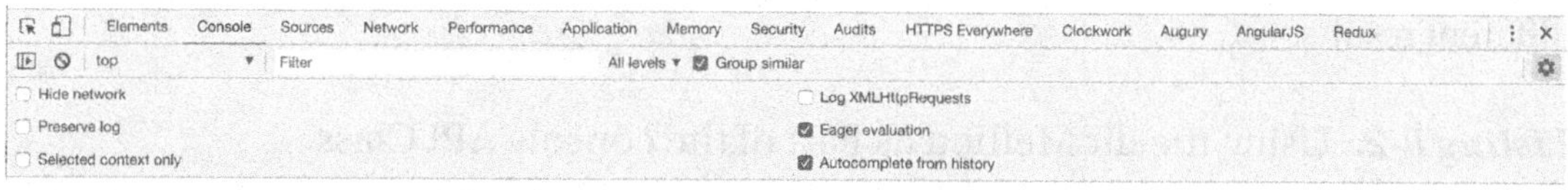

Figure 8-2. Displaying the Console settings

The console object has a few methods that are useful for understanding what is happening with your code as it is being executed. For example, the `count` method tracks how many times a function has been called from the same source. In this case, it's the same a button click. See Listing 8-1.

Listing 8-1. Using the count Method as Part of the console API Class

8-1.html
```
<button id="myButton">Click Me</ button >
```

8-1.js
```
function myCount(evt){
    console.count(evt);
}
document.addEventListener("DOMContentLoaded", () => {
    document.querySelector("#myButton").addEventListner("click", myCount);

});


//result [object MouseEvent]: 1..2..3
```

This example waits for the `DOMContentLoaded` event to happen. It then looks at the document and finds the button by its ID and assigns an event listener to it.

When the button is clicked, the count method tracks how many times the function that is associated with the button click is called. So, without creating a variable in your code, you can see that this function gets called a certain amount of times.

The dir method takes an object and prints it out in the console. Here you can click to see all the properties and methods displayed for an object, including any child properties and methods.

Listing 8-2 takes the code from Listing 8-1 and uses the dir method to achieve different results.

Listing 8-2. Using the dir Method as Part of the console API Class

8-2.html
```
<button id="myButton">Click Me</ button >
```

8-2.js
```
function myCount(evt){
    console.dir(evt);
}
document.addEventListener("DOMContentLoaded", () => {
    document.querySelector("#myButton").addEventListner("click", myCount);

});
```

This code lets you look at all the properties and methods that come with the MouseEvent. This is similar to using console.log where you can see all the properties and methods of the objects that you are working with. See Figure 8-3.

```
▼MouseEvent
    altKey: false
    bubbles: true
    button: 0
    buttons: 0
    cancelBubble: false
    cancelable: true
    clientX: 56
    clientY: 12
    composed: true
    ctrlKey: false
    currentTarget: null
    defaultPrevented: false
    detail: 1
    eventPhase: 0
    fromElement: null
    isTrusted: true
    layerX: 56
    layerY: 12
    metaKey: false
    movementX: 0
    movementY: 0
    offsetX: 47
    offsetY: 2
    pageX: 56
    pageY: 12
  ▶ path: (5) [button#myButton, body, html.no-js, document, Window]
    relatedTarget: null
```

Figure 8-3. *Displaying the methods and properties of the MouseEvent object*

A method that is similar to calling `console.log` is `dirxml`. This method returns an object, but instead of displaying all the properties and methods as a JavaScript object, it displays it as a tag-based XML document.

Listing 8-3 shows the `dir` and the `dirxml` methods. In this example, the function `myCount` displays `dirdxml` results first and then the results of `dir`. See Figure 8-4.

Listing 8-3. Using Both the dir and dirxml Methods

```
8-3.html
<button id="myButton">Click Me</ button >
8-3.js
function myCount(evt){
    console.dirxml(document);
   console.dir(document);
}
document.addEventListener("DOMContentLoaded", () => {
    document.querySelector("#myButton").addEventListner("click", myCount);
});
```

```
▼#document
    <!doctype html>
    <html class="no-js" lang>
      ▶<head>…</head>
      ▶<body>…</body>
    </html>
  ▼#document
    URL: "file:///Users/asciiba/Documents/projects/apress/intro-to-front-end-development/chapter8/8-6.html"
    ▶activeElement: button#myButton
     alinkColor: ""
    ▶all: HTMLAllCollection(10) [html.no-js, head, meta, meta, title, meta, meta, body, script, button#myButton, description: meta, viewport: meta, myButton: button#myButton]
    ▶anchors: HTMLCollection []
    ▶applets: HTMLCollection []
     baseURI: "file:///Users/asciiba/Documents/projects/apress/intro-to-front-end-development/chapter8/8-6.html"
     bgColor: ""
    ▶body: body
     characterSet: "UTF-8"
     charset: "UTF-8"
     childElementCount: 1
    ▶childNodes: NodeList(2) [<!DOCTYPE html>, html.no-js]
    ▶children: HTMLCollection [html.no-js]
     compatMode: "CSS1Compat"
     contentType: "text/html"
     cookie: ""
     currentScript: null
    ▶defaultView: Window {postMessage: ƒ, blur: ƒ, focus: ƒ, close: ƒ, frames: Window, …}
     designMode: "off"
     dir: ""
```

Figure 8-4. *Displaying the results of the dir and dirxml methods from the console API*

Figure 8-4 shows that the first level of results displays the document object in an HTML/XML format. You can see the hierarchy of all the tags and click though them.

The second level shows all the methods and properties of the document object. In this case, it is more like looking at a JavaScript object, which makes it more difficult to understand the hierarchy than the first example.

There may be times when you have a few things you want to log, but just using the log method means you need to scroll though the results in the console to find them all. This is where you can use a combination of the group and groupEnd methods. You can take the results of a log and group them together. It is important to remember that to end the group, you need to call the groupEnd method.

Listing 8-4 shows how to take the properties of an object and group them together. This gives you more context when looking at the results in the console.

Listing 8-4. Using the group and groupEnd Methods to Group the Results of the log Method

8-4.js
```
let insocAlbums = {'first': 'Information Socieity', 'second'': 'Hack',
'thrid': 'Peace and Love Inc.'};

function groupBand(albums){
    console.group("Album List");
    console.log('first:' , albums.first);
    console.log('second:' , albums.second);
```

```
    console.log('thrid:' , albums.third);
    console.groupEnd();
}
document.addEventListener("DOMContentLoaded", () => {
     groupBand(insocAlbums);
});
```

In this example, you have an object called `insocAlbums`. You want to see properties of this object grouped together. The next function, `groupBand`, looks at individual properties of the object passed over and prints them in the browser console.

The important difference here is that you explicitly group these items with a title and specify an end to the group. Figure 8-5 shows the results.

You can now see all the items you are interested in from the object grouped together. You can click the group title and expand the list.

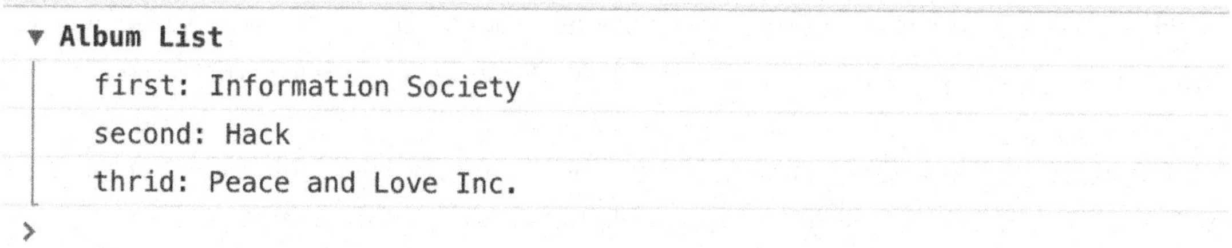

▼ **Album List**

    first: Information Society

    second: Hack

    thrid: Peace and Love Inc.

>

Figure 8-5. *The results of using the group and groupEnd methods of the console API*

The last method I will cover in this section is the `table` method. As the name suggests, it displays the results in a nice table on the console. Let's take the last example and display it as a table. See Listing 8-5.

Listing 8-5. The table Method

8-5.js
```
let insocAlbums = {'first': 'Information Socieity', 'second'': 'Hack',
'thrid': 'Peace and Love Inc.'};

function groupBand(albums){
     console.table(albums);
}
```

```
document.addEventListener("DOMContentLoaded", () => {
    groupBand(insocAlbums);
});
```

The `table` method displays all the properties and methods of an object in a nicely formatted table. Figure 8-6 shows an example.

Figure 8-6. *The results of using the table methods of the console API*

You can see that the results are very similar to what you get with the `group` method. One of the nice things is that you do not need to do any work to make this happen.

This was an overview of some methods available to you via the console panel. For the most part, these methods help you see the values of the objects you are working using.

There may be times when you want to get a better understanding of how the code is being executed inside the browser and how the values of the variables are changing while that code is being executed. The console panel can be a big help, but there is another panel that can give you more detail.

The Sources panel can help you do things like pause the program and let you see what is going on with your code *while* the code is running. Let's take a look at the Sources panel.

The Sources Panel

The Sources panel has three sections. The first is the *file navigator.* It lets you inspect any of the files that are part of your website.

Once a file is selected from the file navigator, you can use the *code editor* to see the contents of that file and make some changes that will be reflected in the browser in real time.

The third panel is the JavaScript debugging panel. This panel lets you do things like watch the value of variables over time. You can also see the value of all the variables currently in scope as the program executes.

In the next example, you will use something similar to what you were working with before. The basic format will be the same. There will be a button to click, but the difference is that this button will make a call to a web service and return some data. Here, you can use the Sources panel as a way to understand how the browser is executing the code.

First, you need to understand the code. Take a look at Listing 8-6.

Listing 8-6. Using the `fetch` method to return data from a webservice

```
8-6.js
let jsonResults;
function getData(){
        fetch('https://jsonplaceholder.typicoce.com/todos/)
        .then(response => response.json())
        .then(json => saveData(json)));
}

functdion saveData(json){
    jsonResults = json;
    console.log(jsonResults);
}
document.addEventListener("DOMContentLoaded", () => {
    document.querySelector("#myButton").addEventListner("click", getData);
});
```

In this example, you are doing a few small things differently. Once the button has been clicked, the `getData` function is called. This function calls the `fetch` method.

The `fetch` method makes a call to a remote service, in your case a service that returns some JSON data.

When the results are returned to the browser, you do something called *method chaining*. This is the ability to call one method directly from another. If you have used JQuery, this is a familiar practice.

The `fetch` method returns something called a promise. A promise gives you the ability to wait for a value.

In this instance, because you are making a call to a remote service, the results may take some time to return a value. A promise will let you know when the data is returned to the browser.

When the result is returned, it can be chained to a then method that will tell the browser to run a function that will parse the results into JSON data that the application can use. You then chain another function that passes the data to a different function called saveData.

Interview Questions   What is a promise and how does it work? What is method chaining?

The saveData function takes the JSON passed to it and saves it to the variable jsonResults.

You can use some of the options in the Source panel to inspect how this is being processed. One way is to set what is called a *breakpoint*. A breakpoint stops the execution of code; this lets the debugging environment give you information about what is happening at that moment in time with your code.

If the browser is expanded, the left side should have the JavaScript debugging tools. Under the section called Event Listener Breakpoints, you can look at the mouse events.

By clicking on the arrow, the list can be expanded to show in detail the types of mouse events you can assign to a breakpoint. See Figure 8-7.

Figure 8-7. *The JavaScript Debugging pane*

By selecting the click breakpoint, clicking the button will pause the execution of the program at the first line of the getData function. At this point, the browser is waiting for you to use the debugging tools to tell it what it should do next.

The debugging tools can inform you of everything that has happened up to this breakpoint. Looking at the Scope panel you can see the value of the variable this.

Another way of setting a breakpoint is to do it directly in the code. Using the current example, if you want to know the value of a variable midway through the execution of the function, you can click inside the saveData function. By doing this, you can see the value of something like the jsonResults variable.

If you do not want to have two breakpoints, make sure to turn off the MouseEvent breakpoint.

After setting a breakpoint inside the function, make sure that you refresh the browser and then click the button. The program will again stop, this time exactly where the breakpoint was set. Looking over at the Scope panel, you can now see the current value of the property this is now window.

Above the Scope panel is the Call Stack panel. This panel shows the order of all the functions executed. From the bottom up, you see the getData function is called first and moves up to your current saveData function.

At the very top of the panels is the Watch panel. It lets you add any valid JavaScript expression, including variables, and watch its value over time.

Unlike setting breakpoints, where you get the value only at that exact moment, Watch lets you see the values even if they change. Open this panel, click the plus button, and type in "jsonResults".

Add a breakpoint at line 11 of the application at the console.log method. Your application currently stops at line 10, which is the location of your original breakpoint. You need a way to move to the next breakpoint so you can see the value of jsonResults change. This is a good time to introduce the ability to use the debugger to move through your code. See Figure 8-8.

Figure 8-8. *The deveoper tools give you the ability to navigate though the code, letting you choose if you want to walk though a function or go to the next one*

Starting from left to right, the tools show how you can move though the code when you set breakpoints. These tools are found at the top of all the panels you have been using.

The first icon lets you continue though the execution of the script as is. It just goes on to the next part of the code that needs to be executed. When using a breakpoint, for example, the first button lets you continue or pause the execution of the code.

In the current example, if you want to move to the next breakpoint, you can click this button and it will bring you to the next line of the code. The browser will stop at the next breakpoint and show the value of the updated value of jsonResults.

If your functions are more complex, you may want to go through that function to get a better understanding of what the function is working on. The next example will use some of the other tools in the debugging panel that help you step though a more complex function.

The first thing you need to do is make your function more complex. This next example will take the value from the jsonResults variable and loop through it using the built-in map function.

The map function will give you the ability to go through each item in the array in order and evaluate each value. It will also tell you the current index of that item. It will also return the entire array on each iteration.

Let's take a look at this. If you downloaded the code for this book, open Listing 8-7. If not, follow Figure 8-9.

```
 9  function saveData(json){
10      jsonResults = json;
11      jsonResults.map((value, index, arr) => {
12          console.log(value);
13          console.log(index);
14          console.log(arr);
15          console.log(checkIndex(index));
16      });
17      console.log(jsonResults);
18  }
19
```

Figure 8-9. *Clicking the Step Over button in the debugging panel moves you from the map function to the console.log function*

As you go through the body of the function, you use the console.log method to output the values that have been returned. You also use this method to output the results of a function called checkIndex.

The checkIndex function looks at the current index and sees if it is divisible by 2 and returns a value of either true or false. You'll use this function to work through the debugging tools.

As discussed, the first button resumes the script, letting it run uninterrupted. The next button allows you to step over the next function call.

If you have the Sources panel open, set a breakpoint at line 10. This will stop the application and you can start to see exactly what that means.

As the application is being executed, if you click the button, everything should stop at line 10. If you click the Step Over button, it should bring you to the next line in the function, where you start to use the map method to loop though all the items in the array. If you click it again, it will step over the map function down to the next function in the list, the console.log function.

If you click the Step Over button again, the pointer will go back to line 10. In the next example, you will use the Step Into button to inspect what is happening inside a function.

If you start this over again by refreshing the page and then clicking the button, the debugger will again stop at line 10.

Now if you click the Step Into button, you still move to the next function, where you start to loop though all the items in the array.

If you click that button a second time, instead of moving to the next function you will now move into the details of the current function and start to see the values being processed in the map function. See Figure 8-10.

```
 9  function saveData(json){
10      jsonResults = json;
11      jsonResults.map((value, index, arr) => {
12          console.log(value);
13          console.log(index);
14          console.log(arr);
15          console.log(checkIndex(index));
16      });
17      console.log(jsonResults);
18  }
```

Figure 8-10. *Clicking the Step Into button in the debugging panel moves you into the map function*

As you continue to use the button, you move down the list of items in the function until you reach the next `console.log` function. Using the Step Into button at this point now brings you to the `checkIndex` function.

Until now you have stepped through each item in the `saveData` function. However, the last line executes a new function for you to step through.

You now start stepping though the `checkIndex` function using the same tools to go line by line, inspecting how this function is being executed.

The next button in the list does the opposite of the Step Into button. It steps out of the current function.

In this example, if you are stepping though the `checkIndex` function and you choose to step out, you will be brought back to the `saveData` function that originally called the `checkIndex` function.

The next button on the list is the Step button. This button lets you go line by line though your function and execute everything as it was written.

The last two buttons allow you to deactivate or reactivate all breakpoints in your application and pause any time there is an exception. Exceptions in JavaScript are when an error occurs.

Summary

This chapter explored some of the tools you can use to debug your website. The focus here was on JavaScript but you can also inspect and edit CSS and HTML, and you can emulate different devices to test the responsiveness of your site.

Other tools include a network monitor to see how long it takes for code to come from the server or the amount of time it takes to make a request and get a response. The Performance panel lets you see how fast the code is being executed, and the Memory panel makes sure that your code is using the browser's memory in an efficient way.

All of these tools are on the client side. You have been using the browser to help you understand how JavaScript works and how to debug it.

As your projects become more complex, you may start to add libraries or frameworks to help organize the application and add features that you need. The next chapter will cover how you can take advantage of NodeJS as a client-side developer.

CHAPTER 9

JavaScript and Client-Side Development

In the early chapters, you installed NodeJS and learned how to do things like run a local server. After that, you spent a good amount of time working with the browser and exploring how JavaScript works inside it. In this chapter, I will introduce tools powered by NodeJS that will enhance client-side development.

NodeJS is something that you should be aware of even if you decide not to work on the server side. It has become part of the ecosystem of any developer who works with JavaScript. Tools like the Node Package Manager (NPM) have become an important part of a front-end developer's life.

This chapter will go over exactly what NodeJS (often just called Node) is and how you as a front-end developer can take advantage of it.

What Exactly Is NodeJS?

In order to understand how current JavaScript frameworks are able to perform actions like create files and folders, it becomes important to take a step back and talk about what exactly NodeJS is and why it is an important part of a JavaScript developer's toolkit.

This discussion about Node will be in two parts. The first part, which I will cover in this chapter, will show how Node is important to client-side development.

The next chapter will cover how to use JavaScript and server-side frameworks like Express to put a webserver together.

© Russ Ferguson 2019
R. Ferguson, *Beginning JavaScript*, https://doi.org/10.1007/978-1-4842-4395-4_9

Node on the Client Side

With Node installed, you gain the ability to use current frameworks like Angular, React, or Vue. Packages are libraries of JavaScript code that you can use in any project. They are distributed using a system called NPM.

NPM has a database of JavaScript libraries that are available to developers. If you want to add some type of functionality to your project, you can use the command line and add it to your project.

To use NPM, you first need to have Node installed. If you have not already installed Node, go over to `NodeJS.org` and install the latest stable release.

Some of what I will cover will be similar to previous chapters, but it is worth going over just as a reminder.

When you have Node installed, a common way to work with Node is to use the command line tools. If you are running Windows, there is a console emulator called Cmder. This tool can be downloaded at `cmder.net`. With it and Git installed (found at `https://git-scm.com/`) you can use all the command line options with an interface that is like using Unix or MacOS.

If you are running Windows and already have Git installed, you can also use Git bash as an alternative.

On the Mac or Linux side, you can use the built-in terminal window. If you are using MacOS, there is an application called iTerm that you can use if you do not want to use the built-in terminal.

With Node installed, you can use JavaScript to do things that are not possible in the browser. For example, you have access to the file system; you can also perform networking and data functions.

For the front-end developer, you can use NPM as a way of quickly putting an application together. When working with NPM, you need to create a file called `package.json`; this file keeps track of all the libraries and corresponding version numbers that you are using in your project.

It is possible to publish your package so that others can use it. In your case, you won't be doing that, but it is good to know what options are available to you.

Using package.json for Your Project

To create this file at the command line, type `npm init`. This will start the process and ask you questions about the project you are about to create. You are not going to publish this package; however, the command line interface will ask you questions as if you were. This is why it is important to understand what it is trying to do.

The first question that you must answer is the name of your project. Here is a list of things to keep in mind when you give your package a name (you can find all the details at `https://docs.npmjs.com/files/package.json`):

- Package names can't exceed 214 characters.

- Names can't start with a dot (.) or an underscore (_).

- New packages can't have capital letters.

This is not important if you do not plan to publish the package. To get a good feel for how to name your package if you do plan to publish, take a look at the registry found at `www.npmjs.org`.

The next question is the version number. Both name and version number are required for publishing. If you make changes to the package, then you should make changes to the version number.

All version numbers should be able to be parsed by node-semver. Semver, or semantic versioning, is a standard to help keep track of the version of your project. Here are some of the rules:

- Use a major version number when the changes are incompatible with previous changes.

- Use a minor number when functionality is added that is backwards compatible.

- Use a patch number when backwards-compatible bug fixes are added.

Using this format, all version numbers look something like 1.0.0 (major, minor, and patch numbers).

To continue, press the Return key; this will leave you with the default version.

The application will next ask for the description of the project. This helps people discover the package if they search for it. You can press Return to continue.

The entry point is the file that will be used when you use the `import` or `require` keywords. Using either of these keywords will add that library's functionality to your project. The default is `index.js`.

The test command option is where you can add commands to run any kind of tests on the application. This can include unit and integration tests. For example, you can type `npm run tests` in a continuous integration environment and make sure that the applications test passes before sending the code to run on a server.

Interview Questions   What is the difference between unit and integration tests? Answer: Unit tests check a small piece of code to make sure it does what it is meant to do. Integration tests check if each of these units work together.

Adding a Git repository helps people know the location of the project. This is also helpful if you open source the project and want people to contribute.

Keywords are helpful if you plan on having the project publicly available. They will help when someone uses "npm search." Keywords are an array of strings. In your case, this is a local project. You can hit the Return key and move to the next item.

The author in this case is you. If you want to add contributors, use an array that contains other people. This array can have names, emails, and URLs. Enter your name and press the Return key, or just press the Return key.

If this is a publicly available project, you can put it under an open source license like MIT or Creative Commons. A full list of licenses can be found at `https://spdx.org/licenses/`; in your case, it isn't open, so you can move on.

With these questions answered, you get a preview of what the `package.json` file is going to look like. The last thing you need to do is approve it.

NPM has created a file that you can use to keep track of the libraries that will be part of your application. At its core it is just a JSON file but in context of what you are going to use it for, it will not only know what libraries you are using but also keep track of the version and any dependent libraries you will need to make your future application work.

The next section will show you how to add packages to a project.

Adding Libraries to package.json

You now have a `package.json` file to keep track of both the libraries you want to use and the versions of these libraries for your project. Using this file, you can also do things like run a local server to see your application work. You can also run scripts to help you during the development, testing, and production of your site.

When adding a library to your project, you can go back to the command line and ask for it directly. NPM will find the Git repository and add it to your project. For this example, let's add jQuery to your project and explore how to use it.

Back at the command line, you should be in the same folder as the `package.json` file; type in `npm install jquery`.

This code finds the Git repository with the latest version of jQuery and downloads it to your machine. It also creates a folder called `node_modules` inside that folder, which is a `jquery` folder containing the library you just requested.

The last file that this process creates is a `package-lock.json` file. This file is helpful in making sure the exact versions of all the libraries you have been working with are installed every time.

Interview Questions   Should you commit `package-lock.json` into your project? Answer: Yes. This will ensure that everyone on your team installs the same versions of all the libraries being used on the project.

So far, you created a `package.json` file and added a library to it. At this point, you don't yet have a full working website. The next few examples will show how to use NPM to put a project together.

In one of the earlier chapters, you added a package called `http-server`; this created a zero-configuration way for you to use your current folder as a webserver.

Let's add this package to your project. At the command line, make sure you are at the root of your project and install `http-server` by typing "`npm install --save http-server`".

With this library installed, you can update your script so that you can have `package.json` tell the server when it should run. Since this is just a JSON file, you can open it up in any editor and make some changes to it.

Open the file in any editor. To update the script section, you add a script that starts the server for you. Under the scripts section, add a script called `start`. Listing 9-1 has the code.

Listing 9-1. Updating the package.json File so the Start Script Will Run a Local Server

```
"scripts":{
"test":"echo\ "Error: no test specified\" && exit 1",
  "start": "http-server"
}
```

Now when at the command line all you need to type is `npm start` and that will start the local webserver. To stop the server from running, you can type Control + C.

You have used NPM to download two libraries, but you don't yet have any HTML files to display.

To fix this, you go back to the command line and create a file. Type `touch index.html`, which creates a blank file called `index.html`.

Your newly created HTML file does not have any content inside it. You can fix this by using code generated by a site called `htmlshell.com`. At its default setting, it will give you the basic structure for an HTML site and for now that is all you need.

After adding HTML to the index file, you can start the project again and see your newly created HTML page loaded by your local webserver.

To make this happen, at the command line type `npm start` and this should start the server again.

Open your browser and type `127.0.0.1:8080`. This will tell the browser to look at the local machine (8080 is the default port number; other projects may use a different number to serve web pages on the local machine).

Currently the page is blank, as shown in Figure 9-1. If you like, you can type into body of the document just to confirm that the page is being served.

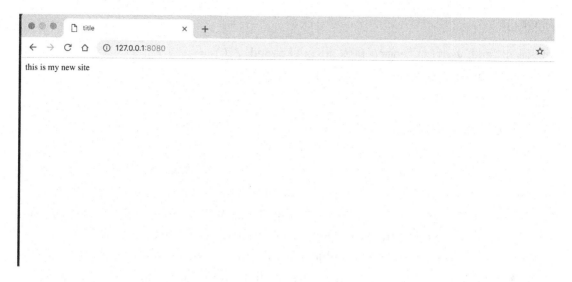

Figure 9-1. *Showing a new HTML page from the local server*

You now have the package.json file starting up your local server and serving an HTML page for you. You need to add JavaScript to your project. If you still have the command line tool open, make a scripts folder to add some JavaScript to the project.

At the command line, stop the server and type mkdir scripts; this creates a folder where you can add your JavaScript. Now you can go into that folder and create new files.

Type cd scripts to change the directory and put you in the scripts folder. Once inside, use the same touch command and create a new JavaScript file.

Type touch app.js inside the scripts folder. This creates a new blank file where you can add your JavaScript commands.

Before you start writing JavaScript, you need to make sure the HTML page is aware that there is JavaScript to work with.

Inside your code editor, open the HTML page if it isn't already open and add a script tag that points to the scripts folder and your newly created app.js file. The code should look like Listing 9-2.

Listing 9-2. Connecting Your HTML Page to the JavaScript File

```
/* index.hml*/

 <body>

<script src="scripts/app.js"></script>
</body>
```

```
//app.js

document.addEventListener('DOMContentLoaded', () => {
    console.log('Document Loaded');
});
```

You add the `script` tag right before the closing body tag so that the rest of the page renders before the browser starts to render any of the JavaScript.

With this in place, you add some JavaScript as a check to make sure that you know your local server is working. You may need to refresh the browser or start the server again to see this work. However, when you open the developer tools and look at console panel, you should see the message "Document Loaded" ready in the console.

This code looks at the `document` object and listens for an event listener called `DOMContentLoaded`. When that event occurs, an anonymous function is fired that gives you a message.

So far, you have a local server running and JavaScript working. However, you have not yet been able to connect your jQuery library to your project.

In order to get that to work, you need to add a module builder. The next section will explain how that works and why it's important.

Introduction to Module Bundlers (Webpack)

You have done a lot of work with the command line so far. You created a `package.json` file that helps you load multiple libraries for your future project. You also added to the script section of this file so you can later use the command line to run a local file server. This ability gives you an idea of what your published site will look like.

Up to this point you have not used the jQuery library that you previously installed in your project. If you remember, when installing jQuery it created a folder called `node_modules` that contained your library.

The browser understands the concept of modules. A module is the ability to have some JavaScript code that will provide some specific function. This separate code can then be imported into the larger project.

As your projects start to get more complex, you will need a few different modules to make everything work. It would be great to add these modules and not add a long list of `script` tags to your document for every module you want to use.

Webpack is a tool that you can use to help use import any library you use in your project and also make sure that the code is compatible with some older browsers.

To get Webpack to work, you need to spend more time at the command line. Stop running your application if you are currently running it and install the Webpack application.

At the command line, type

```
npm install webpack webpack-cli --save-dev
```

This will add the Webpack library to your project. The extra flag, `--save-dev`, is used to add the library to your project but not as something that you will use while you are developing your front-end code.

When looking at `package.json` file, you can see that the library has been added to a new section called devDependencies. This section is only for utilities that help you work *with* the application and not help you *develop* the application. Some of the things that can end up in this section are libraries that help you run things like unit tests or other developer tools.

Now that you have Webpack as part of your development tools, you are going to use it to create your application.

Go back to your `package.json` file and add a new option to the script section. Create a script called `dev` and assign it the value of `webpack`.

It should look like this:

```
"dev":"webpack"
```

After editing this file, at the command line, type

```
npm run dev
```

This will throw an error, as shown in Figure 9-2.

```
WARNING in configuration
The 'mode' option has not been set, webpack will fallback to 'production' for this value. Set 'mode' option to 'development
' or 'production' to enable defaults for each environment.
You can also set it to 'none' to disable any default behavior. Learn more: https://webpack.js.org/concepts/mode/
```

Figure 9-2. *Running a script after adding Webpack to the project*

Sometimes getting an error is disappointing, but in this case it is fine. You know that Webpack is installed and it just need further direction on how to work property.

One of the things that not enough people do is read error messages. Understanding the problem is really important when trying to fix it.

This error is telling you that you need to add more information to your script. Right now, it is defaulting to production mode and this is not what you need at this moment.

Go back to the dev script and update it:

```
"dev":"webpack  --mode development"
```

Webpack has defaults that you need to conform to in order to get your example to work. If you run the script again, you will still have errors.

The structure of your files and folders from the previous example do not conform to the defaults that Webpack wants, so you need to adjust your files to work with Webpack.

Webpack wants the index.js file to be inside the src (source) folder. If you are using code from the previous examples, rename the scripts folder to src and the app.js file to index.js.

If you run the script again, you should not run into the same errors.

When the script is finished executing, it will create a dist folder. This is the folder where all compiled code goes.

When working with tools like Webpack, all the code that gets processed ends up in the dist folder. This includes HTML files and CSS files in addition to the JavaScript files.

When refreshing the browser, the HTML file does not recognize what is happening in the dist folder because the script tag is not pointing to the JavaScript inside that folder.

You need to update the HTML file to point to the JavaScript file inside the dist folder.

One of the benefits to using Webpack is that you do not need to have multiple script tags in your HTML document for every library you want to use.

Back in the HTML page, update the script tag to point to the dist folder and the main.js file that is contained inside.

Just to make sure that everything is working the way you expect it to, recompile the application by going back to the command line and again typing npm run dev.

The first script you wrote in your package.json file was the start script. When running this script, you can use the current folder as a webserver and server the index.html file.

For this exercise to work, you need to have two instances of the terminal window open, one to see the server running and the other to work with Webpack.

In one window, run the script named npm start. It starts the server and tells you what local address to put into your browser to see the site in action.

In the other window, you can continue to update your Webpack scripts.

At this point, you should be able to see your updated script running on your local webserver. With the browser's developer tools open, you should still get the same "Document Loaded" message in the console panel.

All of this setup now gives you the ability to take advantage of NPM.

At the very beginning of this lesson, you loaded jQuery into your package.json file. Now you can add that library into your project without adding it to your HTML page.

Inside the index.js file, add this line at the top:

```
import $ from 'jquery'
```

Then above your current code, add some lines to make sure that jQuery is working. The finished code should look like Listing 9-3.

Listing 9-3. Importing jQuery into Your JavaScript Project

```
import $ from 'jquery';

$(document).ready(()=> {
 console.log('hello from jquery');
});
document.addEventListener('DOMContentListener', ()=>{
  console.log('Document Loaded');
});
```

Run the npm run dev command again and then refresh your browser. Looking at the console panel you should see both messages.

If you are using Chrome and you do not see both messages after recompiling the application, click and hold the refresh button and then select the Empty Cache and Hard Reload option. This should give you the desired result as long as the developer tools are open.

Your application can now make use of other libraries without you needing to add to the HTML file. You can import them directly into your current document and use a tool like Webpack to bundle them in your JavaScript file.

You can upload your HTML file and the contents of the dist folder to a live webserver and it should work exactly the same.

However, for development you have a few immediate problems. First, the application does not know when it should recompile the code. If you make a change, you should not have to then manually tell Webpack what to do.

Another problem is if you want to add Sass (Syntactically Awesome Style Sheets) to your project, Webpack should be able to work with it.

A third problem is if you want to use the latest version of JavaScript. A more current code base would include updates to the syntax that older browsers may not support.

The next section will go over solutions to these problems.

Adding webpack-dev-server

Here you are going to look at some of the problems discussed in the last section.

You know that when any of your source code gets updated, you need to manually recompile your code. This is not an acceptable situation and you need to fix it. You can fix this by using the Webpack webserver. This will replace the server you used before.

Stop the server if it is currently running. Go back to the command line and install the Webpack server. Type

```
npm install webpack-dev-server –save-dev
```

When the install is finished, you can see that the package.json file has been updated.

Now that it has been updated, you can update your original start script, telling it to use the Webpack dev server and not the http-server server.

Back in your development environment, update the start script by typing

```
webpack-dev-server –mode development --open
```

Here you are directing your script to use the webpack server and adding the flag -–open. This flag will open the default browser and load the index page.

The added benefit to this is when you make changes to the files, it will automatically update and refresh the page. This will give you an updated version of the page every time you make an edit.

To test this, make a change to the JavaScript page and save the file. You should see the terminal window update and the browser refresh the page.

You now have the default configuration for Webpack working. Your development server is running, and it will recognize when a file has been updated in your application.

When a file changes, Webpack will recompile the code and refresh the browser so you can see the latest version of the site as if it was being delivered by the server.

JavaScript is a language that is always changing. With this change comes the problem that not all browsers have kept up. Depending on the project, you may need to support older browsers that don't have the abilities you desire.

The next section will introduce Babel.js as a way to solve this problem. It lets you write JavaScript that is up to date and yet still has the backwards compatibility you need to work within the project's needs.

Adding Babel.js

Babel (found at `https://babeljs.io/`) is a tool that you can use when you want to use the most advanced features of JavaScript and still support browsers that may not yet support these features.

It is easy to add this feature to your project. Now that you have Webpack working, you just need to add a few configuration files so that Webpack knows that it should process all of the JavaScript though Babel.

The first thing you need to do is go back to the command line and add Babel to your project. At the command line, type

```
npm install @babel/core babel-loader @babel/preset-env –save-dev
```

This one line will install three parts of Babel:

- Babel core

- Babel loader

- Babel preset environment where you can then compile ES6 code to older versions of JavaScript

The next step is to configure Babel. The way you are going to configure Babel is by using the `.babelrc` file. If you have used Git before, you might be familiar with this. When there is a dot in front of the file name, the file is hidden from the operating system. You may need to change the settings of your operating system to see these files.

If you are at the command line, you can create a blank file with this name by typing `"touch .babelrc"`. This file is usually found at the root of the user directory.

You may need to update your operating system settings to see these files. Open the .bablerc file and add the code from Listing 9-4.

Listing 9-4. Configuring the .babelrc File

```
{

    "presets":[
     "@babel/preset-env"
    ]

}
```

This sets up a preset inside Babel. It allows you to use the latest version of JavaScript, without needing to update this file for every update to the language. It also converts the code into a way that will work in the greatest number of browsers.

You now have Webpack set up and you have Babel set up. You need a way to get these two parts to work together.

When running scripts defined in the package.json file, your goal is to have Webpack use Babel to compile your JavaScript. To achieve this, you now need to add a configuration file for Webpack. This will tie the two libraries together.

Up to this point, you have used the default settings, and they gave you a good amount of ability out of the box. Since Babel is not part of Webpack, you need to direct it using a simple JavaScript file.

Create a file called webpack.config.js. By default, Webpack will look for this file. Similar to the other exercise, go to the command line and type "touch webpack.config.js". The result will be a blank JavaScript file that you can use to configure Webpack. This file is usually found at the root of the project.

This config file sets the configuration settings for each library you want to use with Webpack. In this instance, you export a module that has all the settings for Babel.

Add the code in Listing 9-5 to your configuration file and then you can go over the details.

Listing 9-5. Configuring the webpack.config.js File

```
module.exports = {
    module:{
      rules:[{
         test:/\.js$/,
         exclude: /node_modules/,
```

```
        use:{
            loader:"babel-loader"
        }
}]
        }
}
```

This file exports configuration options for Babel. At this moment, Babel is your only configuration setting. In the future, this could be updated to allow Webpack to work with CSS files, TypeScript files, and other file types including images.

Your configuration settings are inside the module object. This object has an array called rules. This array contains the rules that dictate how the loader works. The first line is test and this rule uses a *regular expression*. The regular expression tells the loader what kind of file it should be working with. In this case, it only works with JavaScript files.

The next item is optional. It tells Webpack not to look at certain folders. Here you exclude the node_modules folder. It makes sense to ignore this folder because it is not part of your application code.

The last option in your example is called use. A mandatory option under this option is loader. A loader must always be a string. Your loader is what connects Babel to Webpack. It will now look at all the JavaScript files in your project and refer to the Babel configuration file so it knows what to do with these files.

With JavaScript being processed by Webpack, you find the results inside the dist folder.

For now, your HTML page isn't being processed. You can add a plugin to Webpack that will make sure that your HTML file will be optimized and also end up in your dist folder.

The next section will expand on what you have done here and show how to use Webpack to optimize both your HTML and CSS files.

Adding HTML and CSS Loaders

In order to get the first part of this to work, you need to add the HTML Webpack plugin. In addition to adding this plugin, you must also add the loader that will be responsible for loading the HTML file for processing.

Using the command line, you can add both the plugin for Webpack and the loader by typing in the following:

```
npm install html-webpack-plugin html-loader –save-dev
```

When this line is executed, the package.json file is updated. This gives you the ability to update your configuration file to use both the plugin and the loader.

The first thing you need to do is require the HtmlWebpackPlugin to work with Webpack. Using require is similar to importing. With it, you add the features to the config file for it to work with Webpack.

Once that has been established, you update the roles for how the loader is going to work. The rules tell Webpack that it needs to load all HTML files and optimize them.

The last thing you need to do is add a *plugins* section. The array in the plugins section will have as its first element the HtmlWebpackPlugin.

The object passed to this function contains two properties: the HTML template (this is the original file that you have in the src folder) and a property that determines both the path and the file name of the HTML file. For now, keep the defaults and continue to call it index.html. This adds the processed HTML file in the dist folder.

At this time your file should look like Listing 9-6.

Listing 9-6. Adding the HtmlWebpackPlugin to webpack.config.js

```
const HtmlWebpackPlugin = require("html-webpack-plugin");
module.exports = {
    module:{
        rules:[{
            test:/\.js$/,
            exclude: /node_modules/,
            use:{
                    loader:"babel-loader"
        }
            }]
},
{
 test:/\.html$/,
use:[
     loader:"html-loader",
      options:{minimize:true}
   ]
}
},
```

```
    plugins:[
new HtmlWebpackPlugin({
    template:"./index.html",
    filename: "./index.html"
    })
    ]
}};
```

With this now in place, running the build script now adds the index.html file to the dist folder.

You now have Webpack processing HTML and JavaScript files. The optimization ensures that the output works in as many browsers as possible.

The one thing that you are missing is CSS. CSS on its own is not a programming language but by using something like Sass, you can use features that are similar to a programming language.

For example, if you want to reuse a color in multiple places, Sass helps you create a variable that holds that current color value. Once the Sass or SCSS files are compiled, they are just CSS files that the browser understands and can be used in your project.

In order to use Sass in your project, you need to add a few loaders to Webpack so it can convert the Sass to CSS.

At the command line, type the following:

```
npm install --save-dev style-loader css-loader node-sass mini-css-extract-plugin sass-loader
```

The package.json file should be updated with references to the libraries that have been downloaded. The next step is to configure Webpack to take advantage of these new updates.

With these new abilities added to your project, you can now update Webpack to take advantage of them. You need to update the webpack.config.js file so that your JavaScript files can import SCSS files and apply styles.

To have this work, the format is exactly the same as the other examples. You add both a *test* and a *use* section to the object array that will take care of how you work with SCSS files. Your webpack.config.js file should look like Listing 9-7.

Listing 9-7. Adding the Sass Features to webpack.config.js

```
const HtmlWebPackPlugin = require("html-webpack-plugin");
const MiniCssExtractPlugin = require("mini-css-extract-plugin");
modules.export = {
    module:{
       rules:[
          test:/\.js$/,
          exclude: /node_modules/,
          use:{
                loader:"babel-loader"
         }
            ]
     },
     {
     test:/\.html$/,
     use:[
         loader:"html-loader",
         options:{minimize:true}
        ]
     },
     {
     test:/\/scss$/,
     use:[
         "style-loader",
         "css-loader",
         "sass-loader"
        ]
}
},
 plugins:[
new HtmlWepPackPlugin({
     template:"./index.html",
     filename: "./index.html"
     }),
new MiniCSSExtractPlugin({
```

```
        filename: "[name].css",
        chunkfile: "[id].css"
    })
    ]
}};
```

With your updated config file set up, you can now create a Sass file and import it into a JavaScript file.

You can take advantage of Sass by creating a variable that will hold the value of a color and then use that variable when declaring the color of an element. Your Sass file should look like this:

```
// _sass/main.scss
$header-color: #b7cbcb;

.header{
    background-color: $header-color;
    width:100%;
    height: 200px;
}
```

You first define the variable `background-color` with a value, in this case a hexadecimal color. The next time you get to use that variable is when you define the CSS class called `header`.

Now that the `.scss` file has been created, you need to import it into your JavaScript file so that the application can use it.

Going back to your original `index.js` file, you can add this line to the top:

```
import './_scss/main.scss';
```

You have most of this working; the last part is to tie it to an HTML element.

Open the `index.html` file and add a `div` tag and, when adding the `class` attribute, give it the value of `header`. It should look like this:

```
<div id="app" class="header"></div>
```

It is fine that there is nothing inside the `div`. You just want to see the effect using Sass with your application.

117

With all of this done, you can go back to the command line. If you are not running the local server, type

```
npm start
```

This should run the local Webpack server and compile all of your code including the .scss file and turn it into CSS.

The browser should look like Figure 9-3.

Figure 9-3. *Compiled Sass being rendered in the browser as CSS*

Summary

Your project now has the ability to import external libraries, automatically update when files are changed, and output JavaScript that can work on as many browsers as possible despite being writing using the latest JavaScript development techniques.

You are also using Sass, which means your styles work in as many browsers as possible. You get these features because you are using NodeJS as your base. Webpack uses Node to give you a local server to use. Your scripts tell the server to watch the files so that the page will refresh as changes occur.

This is just the beginning of how you can work with Node on the client side. Node is the building block for a large amount of client-side tooling. For example, using the latest version of Angular, you can use the command line to build out a bare bones application.

React has a similar tool called `create-react-app`. Either tool will do a lot of the work for you because Node has access to the file system and can create files and folders for you.

This is not the end of all the things you can do with Node. There is a whole new area you can explore. Node also gives you the ability to use JavaScript to run an application server. The next chapter will explore the Express framework and how you can use it to not only serve web pages but to also access data from a database.

CHAPTER 10

JavaScript and Server- Side Development

In the last chapter, you used NodeJS as a way to help with client-side development. The tools that you used were all powered by Node. The ability to create files and convert languages like Sass and advanced JavaScript into something your browser can understand would not be possible without Node.

This chapter will take this idea and expand on it. You will use Node as a web server. Not just a local server, which you did in the last chapter, but a full-blown production server.

To accomplish this, you will use most of the tools from the last chapter. At the command line, create a folder, go into that folder, and use NPM to create a new `package.json` file. Your commands should look something like this:

```
mkdir nodeProject
npm init
```

At this point, you will be asked questions that will be used to construct the file. For a detailed breakdown of all the options, refer to the previous chapter.

For this exercise, you can skip though the options by just pressing Return and accepting the results. At the end, add the Express framework to the project. You do this in the exact same way as you did for your front-end project. At the command line, install Express and save it as a dependency:

```
npm install express –save
```

This will update the `package.json` file and give you the ability to use Express.

© Russ Ferguson 2019
R. Ferguson, *Beginning JavaScript*, https://doi.org/10.1007/978-1-4842-4395-4_10

Basic Express Setup

With your setup done, you can now create some files that will tell Express to start, listen for your requests, and return a string. This is a "Hello World" example. At the command line, create a file called app.js. This is your starting point.

Inside this file, require the Express framework, start the application, listen for requests, and return a response. Listing 10-1 shows the code.

Listing 10-1. Setting Up a Basic Express Server

```
//app.js
const express = require('express');
const app = express();
const port = 3000;

app.get('/', (req, res) => {
   res.send("Hello World");
});

app.listen(port, () => {
  console.,log(`Running on port ${port}!`);
});
```

Your file now has all the basic components for a web server. You can listen for a request from the browser. That request sends a response with the text "Hello World." All of this is on port 3000. To see this in action, go back to the command line and type

```
node app.js
```

This tells Node to look at the file app.js. This file then executes the code and starts running the Express server. Now if you open your browser and type localhost:3000, it should look like Figure 10-1.

Figure 10-1. *Starting up a simple webserver with Node and the Express framework*

The code you added to your application allows the server to run on port 3000. This is important because if you choose a different number, you will not get a response back from the server. Make note of this because other applications use different numbers for development. The default number for web servers is 8080.

Adding nodemon and Routes to the Express App

In the last chapter, you added a feature where the site refreshed every time a file was updated. This made development easier because you did not have to stop and manually recompile the application after every change.

To do this with your Node application, you need to add a library called nodemon. It provides similar functionality. To install it, type this at the command line:

```
npm install -g nodemon
```

You use the -g flag when installing the node monitor to make sure it is available globally. Once installed, you can use this library anywhere in your hard drive.

With this library installed, you can update your package.json script so that nodemon will be used in your development. The start script should now look like this:

```
nodemon app.js
```

This will watch your application and restart the server as you make changes to files.

Now that you don't have to manually restart the server every time you make a change, you can now expand your application.

The first way to expand your application is to create something called a *route*. A route is a path on the server that returns things like HTML pages.

For example, in the first exercise, just look at the root of the server. If you want to have a route called `localhost:3000/users`, currently it would throw an error saying that it cannot "get" users. To fix this, you need to create a route. The next section will explain how to do so.

Creating Routes with NodeJS

Adding routes to your site will set up what kind of actions you would like the server to do. To get a full understanding of how routes work, let's first explore how HTTP works and then how it works in relation to your route. With that full understanding you can get into the code.

HTTP (Hypertext Transfer Protocol) has a request-response model. The browser makes a request of the server, and the server then responds with a resource. This resource usually consists of an HTML page but can be other types of data.

HTTP has a series of methods or verbs that describe the type of action that needs to be performed.

Most of the time when browsers make a request of the server, they just want to "get" information. GET is one of the verbs used when you want to retrieve data from a server. Here is the list of verbs:

- GET: Requesting data from a resource

- POST: Requesting the server to create a resource in the database

- PUT: Requesting the server to update a resource. If the resource does not already exist, then create it.

- DELETE: Requesting that a resource is removed from the database

With this understanding under your belt, you can now come up with examples of what a route will look like when using any of these HTTP verbs.

In the next example, you will start big and go into more detail. If you want information on every state in the United States, a route will look like this:

```
localhost:3000/states
```

Here you make a GET request and ask for information on all the states. Depending on how the database is set up, if you want information on the 11th state (New York), the route will look like this:

```
localhost:3000/states/11
```

In both of these examples, the resource that you are referring to is states. You know that someone on your team has created information about states in a database.

The choice to keep it "states" and not "state" gives you flexibility. For example, the second route narrows down that you want to look at the 11th state.

To extend this, what if you want to delete all the information about the 11th state? The path will be the same, but you will send a DELETE request.

If you want to get all the borough information in New York, your route will look like this:

```
localhost:3000/states/11/boroughs/
```

If you just want to know about Brooklyn, the route will look like this:

```
localhost:3000/states/11/boroughs/3
```

You now have a common language describing how to access items in the database. Formatting routes like this gives you the ability to create, read, update, or delete information. This is commonly referred to as CRUD.

So far, I have discussed what is commonly described as REST services (Representative State Transfer). With this in mind, you can make requests of the server to perform operations on the database. Now let's look at how to implement this with Node.

Using the previous example, creating routes is not very hard. If you want to make a GET request, it will look like Listing 10-2.

Listing 10-2. Creating a GET Route Using Node

```
app.get('/states/, (req, res) => {
    res.send("This is the States Page");
});
```

Here you see that when a route has been requested, Node will run a function and send a response.

Now that you have a baseline for how Node will work with HTTP verbs, the other functions will be very familiar. See Listing 10-3.

Listing 10-3. Using the Other HTTP Verbs with Node

```
app.post('/states/, (req, res) => {
    res.send("This is the States Page POST request");

});

app.put('/states/, (req, res) => {
    res.send("This is the States Page PUT request");

});

app.delete('/states/, (req, res) => {
    res.send("This is the States Page DELETE request");

});
```

You now understand how to use HTTP verbs with Node. Listing 10-4 shows how to serve an HTML page that lives inside the states folder.

Listing 10-4. Setting the Path to Load HTML Pages

```
//app.js
const express = require('express');
const app = express();
const path = __dirname + '/views/';
const port = 3000;

 app.get('/states, (req, res) => {
    res.sendFile( path + 'states/index.html');

});

app.listen(port, () => {
    console.log(`Running on port ${port}`);
});
```

This example shows how to receive a request from the browser and then send a HTML file back to the browser. This example works because you create a views folder and within it a subfolder called states. That folder holds the HTML page.

The use of __dirname gives Node the path of the current running file. In this example, you start at the root and add the views folder. From there, when the route is requested,

Node can run a function that looks at the states folder and sends the states.html back to the browser.

Now that you have an understanding of how routes work and know how to send back either a response or an HTML page to the browser, let's talk a look at how to send data from a database back to the browser.

Setting Up a Local Instance of MySQL

In the last section, I introduced the idea of REST services using a combination of the path to the server and the HTTP verbs to describe what needs to be done with the data.

In some instances, returning a HTML page is exactly what is needed. Some information is static and does not need to refer to information inside a database.

There are other instances where you may be developing something like a single page application (SPA). In these instances, you do not load individual pages depending on the path. Using libraries like React, Angular, or Vue, the application will work out how the routes work and not use the server.

When working in environments like this, the path of the web service becomes very important to the front-end application. The route will determine how the application makes request and how it retrieves information. Web services often are found on a different server than the front-end application.

In this section, you will create a local database, add some data, and make it available as a web service though Node. First, you need to download and install a database.

MAMP/WAMP (MacOS/Windows, Apache, MySQL, and PHP) is a one-click stack of open source software. The individual parts are put together so you can have a simple installation and build a website without needing to configure everything.

Each part of the stack could be a book on its own, but for your purposes, you are only going to look at the MySQL database.

This stack does come with a PHP tool called PHPMyAdmin that will let you edit the local database. There are also applications that you can download that can be used to help edit and update the database without needing to know a whole lot of SQL (Structured Query Language). Some of these tools include Sequel Pro on the Mac and SQL Pro on Windows.

With the package installed, you can then launch the servers. This will open your default browser window with a Welcome to W/MAMP page. With that open you can now access the MySQL database.

You need to create a database to work with. I won't get into all the details about how databases work. What you will do is create a simple table and use Node to create a simple API that will allow you to create, retrieve, update, and delete your data.

In order to understand what a table is, it may help to think of it like using a spreadsheet. When using a spreadsheet all of your information is separated into rows and columns. A database works with a similar setup. In a table, each column is used for a certain type of data and each row consists of the data you are working with.

Use whatever tool you have available to create a database. Sequel Pro has an option that will let you add a database. For your example, name it `api`. Once the database has been created, the next thing to do is to create a table to hold your data. Your script will create a table called `boroughs`. That script should look like Listing 10-5.

Listing 10-5. A SQL Script to Create a Table Called boroughs

```
CREATE TABLE `boroughs` (
  `id`      int(11)      unsigned NOT NULL AUTO_INCREMENT,
  `name`    varchar(30) DEFAULT ",
  `state`   varchar(50) DEFAULT ",
  PRIMARY KEY (`id`)
) ENGINE=InnoDB DEFAULT CHARSET=utf8;
```

The most important thing to know about this script is that it is creating a table called boroughs and this table will have columns called id, name, and state. See Figure 10-2.

Figure 10-2. *Running SQL script to create table*

There should be an area where you can add a query. Once you add it, run the query and create the table.

With the table created, you need to run one more script so you can have just a little data to work with. This script will insert Brooklyn as a name and New York as a state. You do not add a value for ID because that field is set to auto-increment. With this set up, every time you add a new item into the database, it will gain a unique number.

Here is what an insert script should look like:

```
INSERT INTO `boroughs` (`id`, `name`, `state`) VALUES (NULL, 'Brooklyn',
'New York');
```

Now that you have a table with some data, you can go back to Node and work on your API. First, you need to connect MySQL to your Node application.

One of the first things you should do is install the MySQL module to your project. This is just like all the other work you have done at the command line. Add the module by running this command:

```
npm install mysql –save
```

With this installed, it will make it easy to refer to MySQL and access data inside your newly created database.

In section, you quickly set up a database using W/MAMP and you ran a few SQL scripts to create a database and a table inside the database. You are now in a good place to use Node to access data from the database. Node will run queries against the database and return the results to the browser.

It's important to work out how you are going to organize your files. You established that depending on the paths you want to return certain types of data.

The next section will discuss how to create routes with Node and retrieve data from the database.

Returning Data from MySQL Using NodeJS

In the last section, you downloaded and set up a database. You also added some data so you can test your *routes*. Routes are the paths you are going to pass over to Node telling it you want a certain type of data.

The way you set up your project will give you the ability to expand and add other routes, but for this instance you are going to focus on this one route.

You need to create a few folders that will hold your files. Create a data folder and a controllers folder inside your current project.

Inside the data folder, create a file called config.js to hold all your configuration settings for the database.

Inside the controller folder, add an index.js file and a boroughs.js file. With these files in place you can start to code the configuration options so you can connect to your MySQL database.

Inside the config.js file, add the code from Listing 10-6.

Listing 10-6. Configuration Settings for Node to Connect to the MySQL Database

```
const mysql = require('mysql');
const config ={
host:'localhost',
user:'root',
password:'root',
database:'api'
port:'8889'
}
const pool = mysql.createPool(config);
module.exports = pool;
```

The code in this example is similar to how you created the Node server. First, the mysql library is required and assigned to a variable. Then you create an object with all of your configuration settings. After that you create what is called a pool. This gives you the ability to have multiple connections to the database and helps manage those connections. Finally, you export the pool object to be used in other parts of your code.

You now have the ability to connect to your local database. You now need to create a route that will be part of your API to retrieve data.

Your original app.js file is the starting point for your Node application. In previous examples, you learned how to listen for a request and respond to it.

Now you need to have Node capture the request and filter out where that request needs to go. This is possible by using the use method. Open app.js and add the code from Listing 10-7.

Listing 10-7. Having Node Send All Requests That Are Not to the Root of the Application to the Controllers File

```
app.use(require('./controllers'));
```

This code takes all requests from the browser and sends them to the required `controllers` folder.

Before, you created a file called `index.js` inside the `controllers` folder. By default, Node will refer to this file and use it to figure out what to do next.

This example creates one single route; however, you have the ability to add as many as you like. You could have added everything in the `app.js` file. That would have been a simple solution; however, it would have been difficult to scale and test.

Here you make it clear which files will handle each request. Your `index.js` file should look like this:

```
const router = require('express').Router();

router.use('/boroughs', require('./borough'));

module.exports = router;
```

The first line should be familiar since it is what you were using in `app.js` to get Node to start working. Here you add the ability to use the `Router` object. This object performs only routing functions and gives you the ability to add functions for things like authentication.

Now that you have access to the `router` object, you can use the same `use` method to direct Node. You tell Node that every request to `/boroughs` must be handled by the `borough` file.

Here you have been able to narrow down how Node handles routes. From a very high level, you direct it to the index file in the `controllers` folder. Then you figure out the direct route that has been requested. Finally, you handle the details of the request and how to send a response back to the browser.

The `boroughs.js` file checks if the request was just at the root of this route. It then asks the database for everything it has on this subject. The other case is if it makes a request based on the index number in the database. If that is the case, it sends a single result.

In your case, you only have one item in the database, but this is a good introduction for when you both add and update items in the next chapter.

The boroughs.js file needs to be updated. This file should also use the Route object that Node provides. You also get to import the pool object you created earlier in this section and use it to make a request of the database.

Your file should have two methods that look like this:

```
const router = require('express').Router();
const pool = require('../data/config');

router.get('/', (req, res) => {
  pool.query('SELECT * FROM boroughs', (error, result) => {
          if(error) throw error;
          res.send(result);
});
});

router.get('/:id', (req, res) => {
  const id = req.params.id;
  pool.query('SELECT name, state FROM boroughs WHERE id = ?', id, (error,
  result) => {
          if(error) throw error;
          res.send(result);
});
});

module.exports  = router;
```

Starting from the top, you create the Route object. Then you require the pool object that has all the database information.

Now you can start to handle requests that browsers or applications will make of Node. When an application makes the request localhost:3000/boroughs/, your first method will handle that request and make a call to the database.

Here you need to understand a little SQL; using the pool object you use the query method and pass your query as a string.

Capitalization is not necessary when writing SQL; it is more of a formality. SQL commands are often capitalized.

Here you want to select all the columns in the table called boroughs. You know that you want all of them because you use the asterisk as a way of selecting columns instead of asking for each column by name.

After you add the query, the callback function looks for either an error or a result. That function checks for an error using an `if` statement. If no error is found, then it sends the result of the query back to the application that requested it.

The second function is very similar to the first. The important difference is that it looks for a parameter as part of the call. Where the first method just wanted to know if you were making a request of the `/boroughs` route, here you want to know not only if you are making a request of that route but if you want to know the route by index number.

The second function is looking for a variable called `id`; you know this by how the request is set up as `/:id`. By using the colons before the name, you know that this is a variable that an application will pass over to Node. You then need to create a variable to capture that value and use it as part of your query.

Once you have the value, you can add it to your query. In the first example, you have the query and the callback function. In the second example, you add the value of id in the middle, so that the database knows what id to look for.

If the server and database are both running, you can go to the browser and see the results. In each case, you should have a JSON object returned to you. See Figure 10-3.

Figure 10-3. *Receiving a JSON object based on the route requested from Node*

You now have a Node server that you can use to retrieve data from a database. The API you created can give you a single result based on passing the id of item you are interested in, but you can also get all the information in a single call.

Summary

This chapter covered how to use JavaScript on the server. You learned how to use Node and the Express framework to handle requests from browsers and other applications.

You installed MySQL to use as your database. MySQL is one of a number of databases that you can use with Node. The examples introduced some SQL that created a table and added some data for you to use.

Finally, you took advantage of the `Routes` object. You used it to work out the path that was requested of Node. You were only interested in the `/boroughs` path. If it was requested by the browser, Node ran a query against the database and returned a JSON object with the results of that query.

You also figured out how to ask for very specific information. By passing parameters to the server in your URL, your script extracted that information and used it as part of your query.

Now you have the ability to use the browser or an application to retrieve data directly from the database. This will become more important if you develop a single page application. Applications of this nature make requests of the server and update the pages based on the results.

The next chapter will introduce Angular as a way to create a single page application and update or retrieve data from your API.

CHAPTER 11

JavaScript and Application Frameworks: Angular

In the interest of trying to keep this discussion simple, when I refer to application frameworks, I am talking about any library or framework that helps you to develop full web applications quickly. This could include but is not limited to Angular, React, Vue, and Polymer.

Some of these libraries are considered full frameworks, while others are just libraries. The goal of this chapter is not put one against the other or describe the pros and cons of each. The goal of this chapter is to show how you can take all of the knowledge developed in the previous chapters and use it to develop applications using these frameworks.

In the last chapter, you developed an API that sends a JSON object describing boroughs. You used a combination of MySQL and NodeJS to have the server query the database and return the results of that query.

This chapter will cover how to develop a web application using Angular, and the next chapter will cover React. Both applications will be able to access the API developed in the last chapter.

The first half of this chapter will cover how to quickly develop an Angular application using the command line interface (CLI) to generate all the files needed to retrieve data from the API.

Once you are able to retrieve and display your information, you will then create a form that can add or update information in the database.

© Russ Ferguson 2019
R. Ferguson, *Beginning JavaScript*, https://doi.org/10.1007/978-1-4842-4395-4_11

Installing Angular

If you really want to have a good understanding of the Angular framework as a whole, the best place to go to is the project home page (`https://angular.io`).

Since you are going to use the command line interface to develop this application, the next site you should look at is the home page for CLI development (`https://cli.angular.io`).

Using the CLI is very similar to the last few examples when you worked directly with Node.

Open the terminal window if you do not already have it open and use Node Package Manager to get Angular onto your machine.

At the command line, type

```
npm install -g  @angular/cli
```

This command installs the command line tools for Angular on a global level. Once the installation is finished, you can create Angular projects in any folder on your hard drive.

Angular describes itself as a platform for building applications on the Web. Note that we are not talking about AngularJS, commonly called Angular 1. We are only going to discuss the most recent version of Angular, commonly called Angular 2+. At the time of this writing, the most recent version of Angular is 7.

Angular is an open source, TypeScript-based platform led by the Angular team at Google. TypeScript is an open-source language maintained by Microsoft.

What Is TypeScript?

TypeScript is a superset of JavaScript, meaning that you can use the more advanced features that have been built into JavaScript, in addition to using JavaScript as a strongly typed language.

One of the differences between TypeScript and JavaScript is that JavaScript does not force data types, meaning that you can't force a variable to only work with strings or numbers. JavaScript is flexible when it works different kinds of data.

TypeScript also has the following features:

- Interfaces

- Generics

- NameSpaces

- Decorators (experimental feature)

Other languages enforce the idea that once you declare a variable as certain type, changing that type will produce an error.

If you have used languages like Java or Scala, the syntax looks similar. When declaring a variable, you can explicitly direct the compiler to treat a variable to only use a certain type of data:

```
let x: number = 42;
```

This code forces the TypeScript compiler to make sure that any variable assigned to x will be a number. Trying to assign any other type of data will be caught at compile time and will produce an error. Here is an example:

```
let x:number = 42;
x = "Fourty Two" //produces an error
```

The TypeScript language has a compiler that will convert TypeScript into JavaScript. The newly created JavaScript can be understood by a wide range of browsers. As a developer, you can take advantage of advance features in JavaScript that not all browsers understand. An additional benefit of using TypeScript is the ability to find errors at compile time. TypeScript gives you many of the features someone coming from an object-oriented language would expect.

In the next section, you will use the CLI to create an Angular project and have it run in the browser.

Developing an Angular Application

Up to this point, you have been able to install the Angular CLI tools. Using these tools will help you develop an application using the Angular framework. Angular will download all the files needed to construct the application and create all the folders needed to have a basic Angular application.

At the command line, type in this command to make an application called my-app:

```
ng new my-app
```

This one command generates a few questions about how you want to develop your application. You can always update the application at a later date, but for now let's go over some of the questions that the CLI is asking.

The first question is, "Would you like to add Angular routing?" Routing with Angular is just like routing with Node. The idea is to pass a path into the browser that will display a certain part of the site. The big difference here is that Angular will handle the route and *not* the server.

This distinction is important because both applications will try to resolve the route. The server will use the route to find a folder with files based on that route and then try to send a result back to the browser. Because these files and folders do not exist on the server, the result will be a 404 or File not found error.

For your example, let's agree to add this to your application. Type Y at the command prompt and move on to the next question.

The next question is, "Which stylesheet format would you like to use?" The different formats presented are

- CSS

- SCSS

- Sass

- LESS

- Stylus

The first option should be straight forward. The next four are all similar in how they work with stylesheets.

The first two in this list are the most similar and the others are easy to understand after understanding the problems the first two are trying to solve.

Both Sass and SCSS are preprocessing languages, meaning that they will compile down to CSS that your browser will understand. The only real difference is the syntax.

Sass uses indentation to indicate nesting of selectors. Here is an example of the Sass syntax:

```
//sass example
$backgroundColor: #C0C0C0; //silver
.container {
      h1{
  background-color: $backgroundColor;
;      }
}
```

When this code is compiled, Sass knows to make the h1 element that lives inside the container class a background color based on the variable crated at the top of the file,

Sass also extends the language with the addition of nested rules. These rules are called mixins; with mixins, you get the ability to do math in addition to other features.

Files with the .scss extension have a more flexible syntax. This includes writing straight CSS. It also gives you the ability to use features like. Listing 11-1 shows an example of SCSS.

Listing 11-1. Creating a Variable to Be Used Later in Your SCSS File

```
//scss example
$textColor: 'red';
p{
 color: $textColor;
}
```

LESS is also a preprocessor that will convert into CSS. The difference here is that LESS is written in JavaScript and requires Node.

There are minor syntax differences when creating variables. While Sass and SCSS use a dollar sign ($) to create variables, LESS uses the at symbol (@).

The last option in the list is Stylus. Inspired by Sass and LESS, some of the things that make it different from normal CSS are that curly braces and semicolons are optional. Variables do not need to be declared with either a dollar sign ($) or an at symbol (@).

All of these options are valid to manage and scale CSS; for your projects, you can choose whichever you are most comfortable with. In this example, let's select Sass.

When you make a selection, the CLI will then create all the files and folders needed for your Angular project. You should now have a folder called my-app. Go into that folder and start the application type:

```
cd my-app
ng serve
```

Once inside the application folder, you can run the application. When the application is finished compiling, you can see it in your browser by opening your browser and typing localhost:4200. Your browser should look like Figure 11-1.

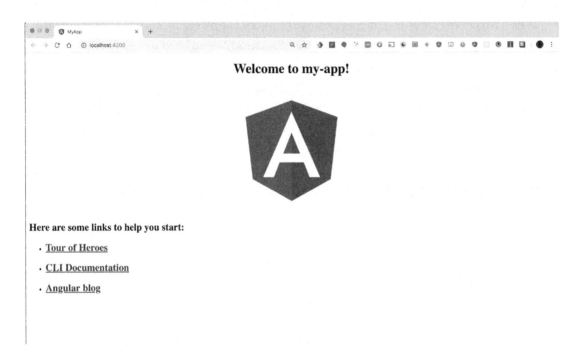

Figure 11-1. *An Angular application running on the local machine*

This is the default page for any Angular app created with the CLI. You can now start to customize this default application for whatever purpose you see fit.

When starting this application, you use the command ng serve; this is specific to Angular. By using a series of commands that start with ng, you can use the CLI to do things like add files, run your test suite, and build the final version for production. It can even update libraries and dependencies on its own. For the full list, type ng help.

Now that you application is built, let's get a better understanding of how it is organized.

Angular's Architecture

Frameworks like Angular and React have a concept of *components*. Components are simply where you put all the HTML and CSS for different parts of the application.

An example of this is a header. A header may have the company logo and a login button. Once a person has been authenticated, the header should show a logout button. All of these features should live inside the header component, and the application logic should determine what should be visible and when it should be visible.

Angular also has a concept called *modules*. Modules in Angular are not the same as JavaScript modules. In this case, modules in Angular give you a place to put all the related code for a certain function. You can use the header as an example. A header module includes all the files needed to make the header work properly in the application.

All Angular applications have a *root* module; this module boots up the application. The `app.module.ts` file lives in the `src/app` folder. It is the module that boots up the application.

In the last chapter, you created an API using Node. You can now create a module that will give you the ability to make a request from Node and display the results.

At the command line, you are going to make a module that you can then build on. This module will soon let you have a component to hold all of your display information. It will also make use of forms and services to connect to your API.

Your first exercise is to create a component with a button that will make a request of the Node server and display the results in your Angular application.

To create a module, type `ng g module boroughs` at the command line. This code creates a new module that you can build on.

Once the command has been executed, you need to get the larger Angular application to be aware that this module is now available. To do that, open the `app.module.ts` file. Here you import your module into the main application module.

Inside the `app.module.ts` file is an `imports` array. This array lets you add your new module to the main application. If you are using an application like Visual Studio Code, you can start to add your module to the `imports` array directly. Visual Studio, like other development applications, will know that you want to add this to the application and automatically add the `import` statement at the top of the document.

The imports section of the `app.module.ts` file should now look like Listing 11-2.

Listing 11-2. Adding a New Module to the app.module.ts File

```
imports: [
  BrowserModule,
  AppRoutingModule,
  BoroughsModule //this is the new module
],
```

Now that the main application is aware of your custom module, you need to add a component to that module. I mentioned that components are your view layer to the application. This is how you get to interact with the application and see the results that come from the database.

To create a component that will be part of the boroughs module, you need to make sure that the files are generated inside your boroughs folder. At the command line, type

```
ng g component boroughs/list-boroughs
```

This creates all the files needed to create this component inside the boroughs folder. It also updates the boroughs.module.ts file, letting that module know that it now has access to the component.

The declarations array is updated when using the CLI to create your component. The declarations array keeps track of all the components that are being used inside this module.

In order for your component to be visible in the browser, you need to create an exports array and add this component to it. See Listing 11-3.

Listing 11-3. The Updated boroughs Module

```
@NgModule({
  declarations: [ListBoroughsComponent],
  imports: [
    CommonModule
  ],
  exports: [
    ListBoroughsComponent
  ]
})
```

Now that the component can be exported, you can use it as an HTML element in your application. Inside the `list-boroughs.component.ts` file is a section called selector. The selector is the name of your custom HTML element.

You can add this element to your HTML page just as if it was any other native HTML element. The Angular compiler will make sure that this element is rendered properly in the browser.

To see this in action, open `app.component.html`. Here you have all of the messaging that you saw on the home page. You are going to remove it and add your new custom HTML element. At the end, `app.component.html` should look like Listing 11-4.

Listing 11-4. Adding the app-list-boroughs Component to the app.component. html File

```
<!--The content below is only a placeholder and can be replaced.-->
<div style="text-align:center">
  <app-list-boroughs></app-list-boroughs>
</div>
<router-outlet></router-outlet>
```

Once this file is updated you should see the application compile all of the code and show a new result in the browser. The page should look like Figure 11-2.

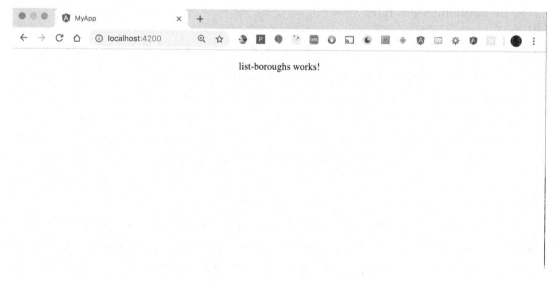

Figure 11-2. *Chrome rendering the updated app.component.html file*

You now have your custom component rendered by Angular. In the next section, you will create a service that will make a call to the Node application and display the results in your page.

Creating an Angular Service

Up to this point you used the Angular CLI to create an application and develop a custom component. All of this is visible in the browser on your local machine without needing to upload to a remote server.

Components serve the purpose of displaying information and dealing with user interaction. Components should not be used to do things like fetch data from the database.

In Angular, you use services to perform actions like fetching data from the database. Services can be injected into any component. This provides the ability to write one service for a particular action and reuse it with different components. You are going to use the CLI to create a service. Your service will first connect to a remote server as a test.

After you know it's working, you will connect to your local machine running the Node application you created in the last chapter.

You are going to use the CLI to create a service. This service will live in a folder called service/borough. The file itself will be called borough.service.

At the command line, type

```
ng generate service service/borough/borough
```

This adds the service folder to inside the src/app folder. Then it adds a boroughs folder; inside that folder, it creates a borough.service.ts file.

With your service created, you can now give your custom component access to it; after that you can configure your component so that it can make calls to remote services.

I discussed the ability services have to be available in multiple components. This is because services can be added or "injected" into multiple components. Let's add your service to the list-boroughts.component.ts file.

Open that file and import the service. With the service imported, you can create an instance of this class by using the constructor method inside the component. Both JavaScript and TypeScript have the concept of classes. When creating a class, you are defining a "blueprint" of how a type of object should work.

Using that blueprint, you can create as many objects you like to suit your needs. When creating a class, you first declare the class and its name. Inside that declaration you define the `constructor` function. This function is used to create or initialize objects inside a class.

In Listing 11-5, you first import the service. Then you create an object using the constructor function.

Listing 11-5. Importing the BoroughService into the ListBoroughsComponent

```
import { Component, OnInit } from '@angular/core';
import { BoroughService } from '../../service/borough/borough.service';

@Component ({
      selector:'app-list-boroughs;,
     templateUrl:'./list-boroughs.component.html',
       styleUrls: ['./list-boroughs.component.sass']
 })
export class ListBoroughsComponent implements OnInit{
  constructor (private boroughService: BoroughService){}
     ngOnInit(){
          this.boroughService.getBoroughs().subscribe((data) => {
          console.log(data);
        }):
    }
}
```

There is a lot to unpack in this code. I have not yet discussed how components work. You have only created them and added the ability to display them on screen. Now that you need to add a service, let's go over in detail how components work and what is going on in this example.

Components represent the visible part of an Angular application. Component classes have something called lifecycle hooks. These hooks are managed by Angular and they let you know what is happening with any component at a given time.

For example, the lifecycle hook you use here is `OnInit`. When used inside a class, lifecycle hooks start with ng so the function you will use is the `ngOnInit` function.

The first line imports the two items needed to make your Angular component work. The first is the component decorator. You can see in this example; the `@Component` decorator is the first thing that makes this different from a regular TypeScript or ES6 class. It lets the Angular compiler know that this class is part of the Angular framework.

Inside this decorator, you create an object that describes to Angular both the visual details and how it will be implemented in the application.

From top to bottom, @Component first describes the selector. This is the custom HTML tag that you used in your other example to make this component visible in the document.

The second element in this object is the templateUrl. It points to the HTML file this component is going to use.

The last section is styleUrls. It points to an array of stylesheets with one file set as the default.

Using the @Component decorator you can now add all the metadata (a term you will see in the documentation) that describes how this component is going to work inside the larger application.

Returning to the first line of the file, the second thing that is imported into the code is a lifecycle event called OnInt. You can see this in action in the class declaration. Your class implements OnInit as part of the class.

This keyword implements in TypeScript is important. You are telling the compiler that this class will use the method OnInit inside the class. If you tell the class that you are going to implement something and then you don't use it in the class, you will get an error.

After you declare your class, you have a constructor function. These functions exist in both JavaScript and TypeScript. Constructor functions can only be used once inside a class. In TypeScript, you can create an object inside the constructor function. In this instance, you create a private object whose *type* is BoroughService.

When you declare something private, it means that other objects cannot access any methods or properties of this object from the outside. There are a few keywords you can use to control the level of access other objects have to methods and properties of the object you are working with; for now, you will just stay with private.

After using your constructor function, you can use the lifecycle method ngOnInit. When the component is initialized, access to the boroughService object is created by the constructor and it runs the getBoroughs method.

You use the subscribe method to tell Angular that you will retrieve any results returning from the service. You assign the results to a variable called data and run a function that will display the results in the browser's console window.

146

You now refer to a function that is part of the service. The getBoroughs function should return a result. At this moment, you have not yet updated the service. Depending on the environment that you are using to write your code, you can use the Control key or Command key (if you are using MacOS) and click boroughService.

This opens that file and gives you access to the service directly. Here you can update your service. The next section will show how you add the ability to make calls to external resources and pass that data back to the component.

Updating Your Angular Service

The last section showed how to use the CLI to create a service and use it inside a component. This section will show you how to have this service access external resources and send the results back to the component to be displayed.

If you used the CLI to create the file, make sure the file is open. You are going to just add a few items to this file to will give you the ability to make calls to a remote API. When you are finished, the service should look like Listing 11-6.

Listing 11-6. The BoroughService Class

```
import { Injectiable } from '@angular/core';
import { HttpClient } from '@angular/common/http';

@Injectable ({
     providedIn:root
})
export class BoroughService {
  constructor (private http: HttpClient){}
     getBoroughs() `Observable<any>{
         retun this.http.get('https://jsonplaceholder.typicode.com/
         todos/1')
     }
}
```

For the most part, the format you are going use is the same as when you created a component. You import other classes into your class. There is a constructor function used to make an object and you add a public method to this class, which will be available to the component for future use.

One of the things used in a service that is similar to your component is the @Injectable decorator. This decorator gives your class the ability to be added or *injected* into multiple components. With that functionality, you can write one service and reuse it.

Inside the decorator is the line providedIn: 'root'. This optimizes Angular's ability to use what is called *dependency injection*. By injecting the service into the root of the application, Angular can then use a single instance of that service and remove the service from components that are not using it. You can also specify the module you want the service to be available in. Once that module has been loaded, that service will be available. In each case, you won't need to add the service to the provider's array in the module.

The second line you need to add to your service is the HttpClient. This lets you make HTTP calls to any remote service. Since you are making a request of a server, you are going to use the REST verb GET. This will let the server know that you only want to retrieve a response and not add or update any information in the database.

Inside that method is the URL that you want to get information from. In this case, you are using a site called JSONPlaceHolder. This site will return some JSON and let you know that a request retrieved a result.

The first line in the getBoroughs method tells TypeScript that it needs to return this line to the class that is calling the method, in your case the ListBoroughsComponent class.

Now that you have the service set up, you need to make one more addition to the application so that you can use your HttpClient class. In the app.module.ts file, you need add the line

import the *HttpClientModule* from *'@angular/common/http'*

In addition, add the HttpClientModule to the imports array.

You now have a service that can be injected into your component. When the component is initialized, it will run the getBoroughs method on the service and print the results in the browser's console. When the method on the boroughService is called, it will make a GET request of the JSONPlaceHolder and return the results.

When you run the Angular application, the browser window should look the same; however, when you look at the console log, you should see an object with the results of your REST call. See Figure 11-3.

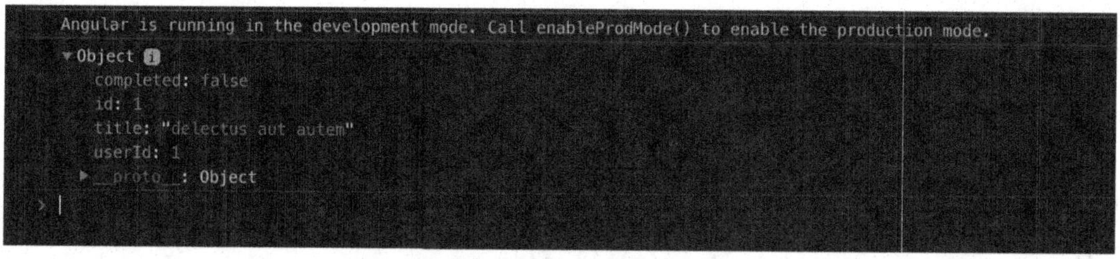

Figure 11-3. *The results of a REST call from the boroughService*

Now that you have verified that there are results returning from a web service, you can have these results displayed on screen.

You will now make minor updates to the component. With these updates, you can display the results of the REST call on the page when it page loads.

Open the component. Here you will create a property to your class. This property will be read by template when it is time to display values in the browser.

You are going to add a property called `results`. You will then assign the data that has been returned from the service to this property.

The code should look like this:

```
private results: any;
constructor (private boroughService: BouroughService) {

}
 ngOnInit() {
        this.boroughService.getBroroughs().subscribe((data) => {
            cosole.log(data);
        this.results = data;
        });
}
```

With your function now able to assign the results to a property in your class, you can display the results on screen.

Open `list-boroughs-components.html`. This is where you add all of the HTML that will make up your component. By default, there is a paragraph with some text. You are going to create three new `div` elements right under that to display the results of your REST call. The updated page should look like this:

```
<p>
  list-boroughs works!
</p>
<div> results.title {{results.title}} </div>
<div> results.Id {{results.userId}} </div>
<div> results.id {{results.id}} </div>
```

If your application is currently running, your browser window should look like Figure 11-4.

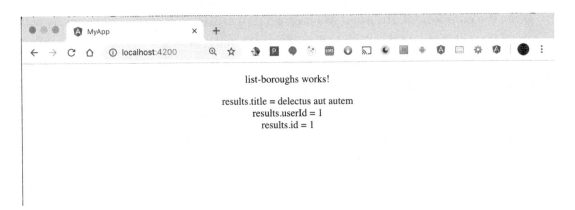

Figure 11-4. *Displaying the results of the REST call in the browser*

You now have the results on screen. This example lets you use a placeholder to get the results back and display them on screen. In the next section, you will take advantage of the Node API you created. Since both your Node application and your Angular application are running on the same machine, you need to develop a way to get them to talk to each other.

Creating a Proxy for Your Local Angular Application

In a previous chapter you created an API with Node. Your API made a request from a MySQL server and returned the results back to the browser.

This section will cover how to get your Angular application to make the same request to your Node server even if they are running on the same computer.

From the perspective of the Angular application, it does not know that it is talking to a separate server. It treats each call as if it was talking to a local server.

One of the benefits of setting up a proxy is you can connect to either a local server like in this example or a remote server while you are developing your application. The proxy file will make sure you are pointing to the right place.

Both Angular and React rely on Webpack for things like converting TypeScript to JavaScript and running a local development server. Webpack also has the ability to let you add a file so you can solve this problem.

On the same level of the package.json file, create a new file called proxy.conf.json. This file tells Angular where to look when it is trying to make a call to a REST service. The call will be rerouted to the server that you specify in this file.

Once this file has been created, add a JSON object that points to the endpoint you want to use, the URL of the server, and if this is a secure call. Your code should look like Listing 11-7.

Listing 11-7. The Body of the proxy.confg.json File

```
{
    "/boroughts/*":{
        "target": http://localhost:3000/boroughs",
         "secure": false,
        "loglevel": "debug",
         "changeOrigin":  true,
         "pathRewrite": {"^/boroughs": ""}
     }
}
```

With this in place, you now need to tell the Angular application that it needs to use this file in development. This way, when you test your web services on the local machine, you can get results in the Angular application.

To do this, you need to open angular.json to update how the application runs when you are in development mode. You can do a search for the name "serve." In the options object, you can add a property right under the browserTarget property. That line should look like this:

```
"proxyConfig":  "proxy.conf.json"
```

Remember to save the file and, if necessary, restart the application.

At a high level, you have enabled the application to know, when the service makes a call to the /boroughs endpoint, to use the proxy and reroute the call to your Node server with the same endpoint.

It's important to remember that even though both your Angular app and your Node app are running on the same machine, they are two separate applications.

The Angular application is using its own server to display the site on the developer's machine. The Node app is also running on its own server. These two applications do not know that the other is running. By using the proxy, you are able to bridge the gap between these two servers and return results from one application to be displayed in the other.

This example works with local development where you can point your Angular application to a local server or even a remote server to retrieve your data; it is not the same when you are deploying the application into production. For more information about how to deploy your application into production, take a look at the deployment section of the Angular documentation at https://angular.io/guide/deployment.

With your proxy now giving you the ability to connect your two servers, you can update the results in your component and display the information returning from your Node server.

In the service, change the URL of your GET method to /boroughs. Without changing anything, you can now look at the console in your browser and see that the Node API sends an array of objects back as a result. In your case, you only have one object inside that array. See Figure 11-5.

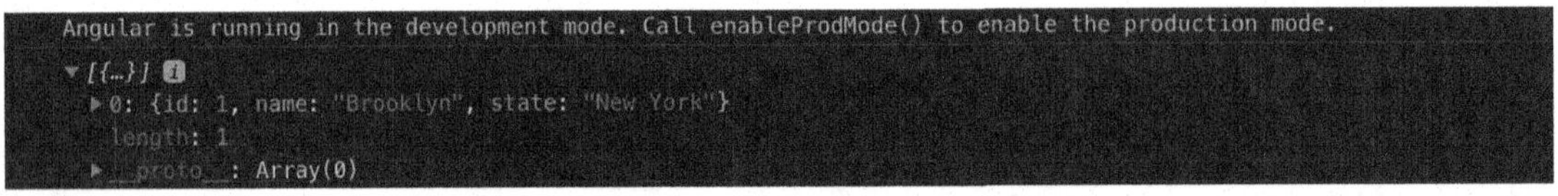

Figure 11-5. *The results of the Node API displayed in the browser console*

The results from the Node server give you an array of objects to work with. In this case, since you only have one result returning, it would be easy to just assign the value of the first element (element zero) to your variable and then display the properties of that object.

While this would work, it does not scale. If you were to add more items in the database, the code in that instance would not account for all the new items that need to be displayed. What you can do is assign a loop to display all the results that are available.

In the HTML file for your component (`list-boroughs-component.html`), you need to update the contents. Here you are going to have Angular look at your array and loop through the results.

For this example, you are going to use the `*ngFor` directive to loop thought the results and display them on screen. When you update the document, the page should look like Listing 11-8.

Listing 11-8. Updated list-boroughs-component.html Using the *ngFor Directive

```
<div *ngFor="let result of results">
 Id = {{ result.id }}
</div>

<div *ngFor="let result of results">
 name = {{ result.name }}
</div>

<div *ngFor="let result of results">
 state = {{ result.state }}
</div>
```

Here you have three instances that will generate `div` tags for each property of this object. The results in your browser should now look like Figure 11-6.

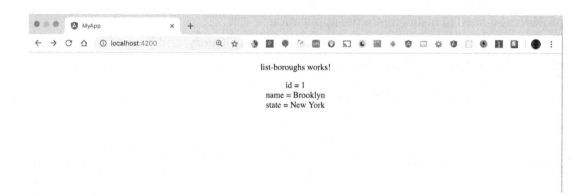

Figure 11-6. *Results in the browser when using the *ngFor directive*

You now have an Angular application that can use a service to request information from a web service. While you are developing the application, you get to use a proxy file to redirect your request to a Node server that can fulfill the request.

When the results are returned to the component, you receive an array of objects. You then use the *ngFor directive to display the list of results.

Now that you have the ability to connect to your service, there are a few things that you should do. The first thing is to work on some of the visuals. You can add Twitter Bootstrap as visual framework to help your application look better.

The last thing that you will do is create a form that will let you create new information in the database. This will require some updates to both the Node application and the Angular application.

First, let's add some styles using Twitter Bootstrap. The next section will show how to add this visual framework to your Angular application.

Adding Twitter Bootstrap to Your Angular Application

Twitter created an open source framework that lets you create consistent visuals for your website. Bootstrap gives you the ability to develop a site that has consistent typography, forms, and buttons.

This section will show how to add Bootstrap to your application. You will also create a form element that will use Bootstrap to give it style. To get a better look at Bootstrap and what you can do with it, go to the home page at https://getbootstrap.com/.

In order to give your Angular application the visual consistency that Bootstrap can provide, you need to install it into the application.

At the command line, use NPM to install Bootstrap, jQuery, and Popper. At the base of your application, type this at the command line:

```
npm install bootstrap jquery popper
```

Once installed, open the `angular.json` file. The styles and test sections need to be updated to refer to the CSS file Bootstrap provides. This can be found in the node_ modules folder. In the scripts section, add the path to the Bootstrap node module. The styles and scripts sections should look like this:

```
"styles":{
    "src/styles.scss",
    "node_modules/bootstrap/dist/css/bootstrap.min.css"
}

"scripts":{
    "node_modules/jquery/dist/jquery.min.js",
    "node_modules/bootstrap/dist/js/bootstrap.min.js"
}
```

Restart the application and you should see the font change. To make sure that this is working, change one of the `div` tags to an `h1` tag. When the application restarts, your page should look like Figure 11-7.

Figure 11-7. *Using Bootstrap's H1 tag in your component*

You now have Bootstrap as part of your application. You can take advantage of the layout and formatting ability Bootstrap gives you.

In the next section, you will create a form. This form will be your way of adding new information in the database.

Creating a Simple Form in Angular and Style It with Bootstrap

You have achieved a lot in this chapter. You created your application, developed UI components, and made a service that will make a call to your Node server. When the call is made, Node will send results back to the Angular application and you can display the results on screen.

Now you are going to add forms to this application. Angular has two different ways of working with forms: reactive forms and template-driven forms. This example will use template-driven forms.

When you gave the application the ability to make calls to a remote server, you had to add the HttpClientModule to the app.module.ts file. This empowered the entire application. For this example, you need to do the same thing with forms.

Reopen the app.module.ts file and import the FormsModule from @angular/forms. Add the imports statement at the top of the document with the others.

```
Import { FormsModule } from '@angular/forms';
```

Also add the module to the imports array. Once finished, do the same thing in the boroughs.module.ts file.

You now can go back to your component and add a form using normal HTML 5 syntax. Your form will be simple. You want someone to enter text into two fields, name and state. You are going to use Bootstrap to give this form some shape. See Listing 11-9.

Listing 11-9. Updating list-borough-component.html with a HTML 5 Form and Using the ngModel Directive

```
<div class="container-fluid">
    <form #boroughForm="ngForm" (ngSubmit)="submitForm(boroughForm.form);">
        <div class="row">
        <div class="col">
            <label for="boroughName">
            Borough Name:
                <input type="text" [(ngModel)] = "model.
                boroughName"  id="boroughName" name="boroughName">
            </label>
        </div>
```

```
    <div class="col">
        <label for="state">
            State:
                    <input types="text" [(ngModel)] = "model.
                    state"  id="state" name="state">
        </label>
    </div>

    <div class="col">
            <button class="btn btn-primary" type="submit">Submit
            </button>
    </div>
     </div>
    </form>
</div>
```

Here you have the template for your form. You are using Bootstrap to create rows and columns, like a grid. You also get to use Bootstrap's CSS class to give your Submit button some style.

Inside the form tag you use Angular syntax to create a variable called boroughForm; right after that, you assign a function to the event onSubmit.

When the Submit button is clicked, this event is triggered and calls the function submitBorough. When this function gets called, you pass over your variable object and the form property. Your function is resolved inside the component.

You also have a form using the Angular directive ngModel. It ties the template to an object inside your component. This object has two properties, boroughName and state.

Now create a class that has both of these properties. You can then connect your code to the template.

At the command line, create a class. This class has two properties that match your template. Type

```
ng generate class boroughs/model/borough
```

This goes into the boroughs folder to create a folder called models and make a file called borough.ts. Inside this class, you need to add two public properties.

Open the file. Before the constructor, add two public properties. It should look like Listing 11-10.

Listing 11-10. Creating a borough Class

```
export class Borough {
        public boroughName:string;
      public state:string;
    constructor (){

      }
}
```

This class gives you a place to save the values that are typed into the form. Next, you import this class into the list-boroughs.component.ts file, just like your other classes, and then create an instance of that class called model to match the template.

Here is part of what the code should look like:

```
import { Borough } from ../model/borough;

private model: Borough = new Borough();
constructor (private boroughService: BoroughService) {
}

submitBorough(value) {
    console,log(value);
}
```

Your class should now have the newly created borough class imported. If you click the Submit button, the results should show up in the console inside the browser. By using the ngModel, you bind the values of your form directly to the object without needing to write any extra code. The result then becomes an object in the console that should contain the values from the form.

There are a wide range of functions you can add to your form. Validation and user feedback could both be added to make sure that someone has typed something in the fields and whatever type fits the format that you need before you submit to the server.

In this instance, you just want to make sure that you are capturing the data from the form and letting Angular have control over it. In the next section, you will pass that data back to your local Node server and update the database.

Passing Information from Angular to Node

You have your front end ready. Bootstrap gives your page structure and the form some style. You gain this without writing any custom CSS.

Using some of Angular's directives you are able to bind data from the HTML template to the Typescript component code and detect when the form's Submit button is clicked.

In an earlier example, you created a service that retrieved data from your local MySQL database. You now need to create a new function inside your service that will send information back to Node. The server will then pick up the data and insert it into the database.

You need to add a library to your Express application so it can accept incoming data. All of your Node examples are based on the work done in Chapter 10. If any of this seems unfamiliar, please refer to that chapter. If you are running Node, you can stop the server. At the command line, add this library:

```
npm install body-parser –save
```

This library allows Node to retrieve data coming into the server when Angular makes a POST request.

I've introduced the concept of REST verbs, such as using GET to retrieve information from the database Now you get to use POST to add new information into the database.

With this library installed into your Node application you can now update your app. js file to take advantage of it. The following is a partial view of the updates:

```
const bodyParser = require('body-parser');

app.use(bodyParser.json());
app.use(bodyParser.urlencoded({ extended: true }));
```

What you now need is to have the server accept a POST call made from the Angular application. To do so, open the boroughs.js file from the controllers folder.

Here you have your original code that responded to a GET request. You can now add the ability to respond to a POST request.

Inside your new function, you will extract the information sent over and assign it to local variables. You will also create an object that will represent the columns and the data being updated. Finally, you will run the SQL query that will update the database.

The updated boroughs.js file should have this code:

```
router.post('/' , (req, res) => {
        let boroughName = req.body.boroughName;
        let state = req.body.state;
        let records = {name: boroughName, state: state};
        pool.query('INSERT INTO boroughs SET ?', records, (error, results)
        => {
    if (error) throw error;
        });
});
```

You create a proxy that allows you to talk to your Node server. For local development you continue to use that proxy to connect to the Node server and pass data from the Angular form. On the Node side, the data that was submitted into the form now becomes a property of the body object.

The properties contain the values that were typed into the form. You can now extract the values and save them as local variables.

Then you can create an object that will match the columns with the values that will be inserted into the database. The last thing is to run the SQL query.

When you get data out of the database, one of the items is the ID of the item in the database. By using INSERT in your query to add new data, the database will automatically create a new ID number for each item that gets added to the database. This is important because it means you don't need to keep track of every item's unique ID.

With your database ready to insert new data and your Node server ready to receive new data, you now need to update your Angular application to send the information over. Open borough.service.ts and add a function called addBorough. It should look like this:

```
addBorough(value) {
  return this.http.post('/boroughs', value,value);
}
```

Just like the GET example, you use the HTTP client that Angular provides to make your POST call. You then take your argument value, which is an object (you can change the name to whatever you like). This object has a property called value and that is what you are sending to the server.

160

You need to update your component so it can send the data to the service. Open `list-boroughs.component.ts`. The most recent function that was added was `submitBorough`. You need to update this function so you can take advantage of the updated service. The function should now look like this:

```
submitBorough(value) {
//console.log(value);
this,.boroughService.addBorough(value).subscribe((results) => {
      console.log(results);
  });
}
```

Now when the form is submitted, the information typed in the text fields will be sent to the server. The server will then add a new record in the database.

When you test the application, you should see that the database has been updated. To make sure the database has been updated, you can take a look at PHPMyAdmin and look up the table that was created before. You can also update the template so you can get all the results that are in the database.

The last update you are going to make is to retrieve the new data into the same page. At this moment, let's move the function that was in `ngOnInit` to a new function called `getBoroughs`. You can take the call as a whole and move it to your new function. It should look like this:

```
getBoroughs(){
   this.boroughService.getBoroughs().subscribe((data) => {
          this.results = data;
   });
}
```

You have a function that, when activated, will make the same call and retrieve all the information in your database. Lastly, you need to update the HTML template so you can get all the results on the screen. This update will take advantage of the previous lesson. You will add a new row that has a new button and when that button receives a click, it will call your new function and update the second half of your template.

The new row should look like this:

```
<div class="row">
    <div class="col-1">
        <button class="btn btn-primary" (click) = 'getBoroughs()'>Get
        Boroughs</button>
    <div>
    <div class="col-11">
        <div *ngFor = "let result of results">
            id = {{ result.id }}
            name = {{ result.name }}
            state = {{ result.state }}
        </div>
    </div>
</div>
```

There are some minor differences in the new row. Bootstrap works with the idea that the screen is broken up into a 12-column grid. Because of this, you add your button in the first column and the results in a column that spans the width of the other 11 columns.

You use the same loop as the previous example. When your user clicks the button, Angular will see that the click event happened. It will call the getBoroughs function defined in your component. You should get the results on screen, similar to Figure 11-8.

Figure 11-8. *Angular inserting and displaying information*

Summary

This chapter covered a lot of ground. You were introduced to the Angular framework. You learned how Typescript is slightly different from JavaScript and how to use it in your Angular application.

You used the command line interface to create a new Angular application, components, classes, and services for your application. You also created a proxy that allowed your Angular application to talk to your node server as if they were running on the same port and not two separate instances.

Using the Express framework, you found a way to connect to your MySQL database and run a query that sent the results back to the Angular application. You also ran a query that inserted data from the Angular application into the database.

Angular provides a long list of functions out of the box that you can use to build your application.

The next chapter will cover how to do some of the same things using React. React does not have all the features that Angular has, but it is a valuable skill to pick up.

CHAPTER 12

JavaScript and Application Frameworks: React

In the last chapter, you were able to create an Angular application and by using a proxy connect to a Node server that had access to a MySQL database. With this setup, you were able to retrieve data and display it on a screen. You also updated the code so you could use the REST verb POST to send data from a form to the server and then see the results after the database has been updated.

This chapter will cover some of the same ground but you will use React instead of Angular. The purpose of this is to show how different frameworks solve problems differently. React gives the developer the freedom to choose whatever libraries they think will address the challenges they have.

Since React has this option, a lot of developers like to put everything together on their own.

Facebook created a way to quickly put a React application together. It is similar to the CLI Angular uses. However, it is important to note that this tool is just to start an application and does not contain the commands to add new files the way that Angular does.

Similar to Angular, if you want to create a React application in any folder you like, you first need to install the application.

At the command line, type

```
npm install -g create-react-app
```

This gives you the ability to create React application in any folder you like.

To create a brand new React application, at the command line, type

```
npx create-react-app my-app
```

© Russ Ferguson 2019
R. Ferguson, *Beginning JavaScript*, https://doi.org/10.1007/978-1-4842-4395-4_12

Interview Questions   What is the difference between npm and npx? Answer: npx lets you execute packages that are in the npm registry without needing to install them, while npm helps you manage packages that are installed either globally or locally on your machine.

This command creates all the files and folders for a basic React application. To start the application, you can type

```
cd my-app
npm start
```

This code starts the application in the same way that the Angular application started. The browser should look like Figure 12-1.

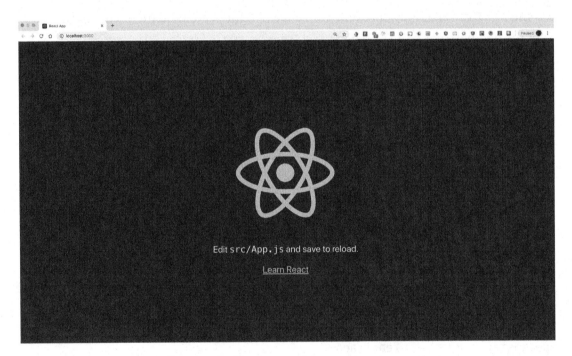

Figure 12-1. *Default screen when using create-react-app*

Now that you have React running on your local machine, you can create components that will let you make a call to the API and display the data on screen.

React describes itself as an efficient, declarative JavaScript library for building user interfaces. With that in mind, you are going to use React to build a component that will retrieve data from your web service.

Since React does not have the ability to create files at the command line, you must make the files you need manually.

So create a folder called components. Inside that folder, create another folder called boroughs and a file called boroughs.js. This is where you will create your React component.

To make sure your new component is going to be rendered by the larger application, there are a few changes you need to make.

Inside the boroughs.js file you will import code that will make sure that this JavaScript class will work with React. The component should look like Listing 12-1.

Listing 12-1. Basic React Component

```
import { Component } from 'react';
export class Boroughs extends Component {
    render() {
                return "this is my component!"
                }
}
```

The syntax of a React component is very similar to a JavaScript class. In order to have this class work with React, you first import the Component class and make sure that the current class extends it.

This class also contains a method called render. It returns the results of all the HTML code that needs to be displayed in the browser.

With your component created, you need a way to show it on screen. To have this component load, you need to update the App.js file.

Each component is treated like a HTML tag. You can import the class you created and have React render it in the application.

Open App.js and import the newly created component. The name of the component is the HTML tag that is used in your application. Your updated file should look like Listing 12-2.

Listing 12-2. Updating App.js

```
import React, { Component } from 'react';
import logo from './logo.svg';
import '.App.css';
import { Boroughs } from '../components/boroughs/boroughs';

export class App extends Component {
    render() {
      return(
              <div className="App">
                  <header className="App-header">
                    <Boroughs/>
                  </header>
              </div>
              );
}
}
```

Now that the file has been updated, the browser should have the updated version. Your browser should look like Figure 12-2.

Figure 12-2. *Default screen rendering a basic component*

React does not have the concept of a service in the way that Angular does. However, React does have the concept of lifecycle methods, just like Angular.

With this in mind, you will create a function that will make the call to your API and display the results in the browser console.

Adding a Proxy and Retrieving Data

Just like the Angular application in the last chapter, you need a proxy to connect this application to the separate Node application.

Making a proxy connection using Create React App is very simple. Inside the package.json file you need to add a proxy section. This will point to your Node application.

Open package.json and add this line:

```
"proxy": "http://localhost:3001",
```

You may notice that in other examples the Node application was pointing to port 3000. By default, React and Node run on the same port, so this will generate conflicts. You must change Node's port. This is a simple update to the App.js file in the Node application.

Chapter 10 has an example of setting up an Express server where you set the port that Node listens to. Refer to Chapter 10 if you need notes on how to update the port for Node.

Open the file for your Node application and change the number of the port to 3001. The updated variable should look like this:

```
CONST port = 3001;
```

In both instances, you need to restart the applications to make sure the changes take effect. You can update your component so you can retrieve results from the database.

React has lifecycle events that will let you know the current state of a component.

Here you will use the componentDidMount function. This will execute when the component has rendered on screen. For a more detailed list of lifecycle methods and how they work, take a look at the documentation at the official React site (https:// reactjs.org/docs/react-component.html).

Inside that function you will use a function called fetch. It is not part of React; it is part of the JavaScript language (https://developer.mozilla.org/en-US/docs/Web/ API/Fetch_API/Using_Fetch). This will make your HTTP call to the server that will be routed to the Node application by your proxy. It will return what is called a *promise.*

A promise is an object that represents the completion of some type of event. In this example, you are making a HTTP request and you expect an answer. The promise will resolve to either the completion of that request, where you get a result, or failure of that request.

This example returns data from the server. The function used inside the then method takes the results, converts them into a JSON object, and returns them back to fetch. The second then method takes the JSON object and converts it to a string to be displayed in the browser console.

Now that you have the results of your API call, and you know that you have a way of looking at the results, the last part of this section will cover how to display the results on screen.

React has a concept called *state.* You can think of state as what the application is doing at this moment. You can set state in a component by creating a state object inside the constructor function.

The next section will show how to create a default state, update the state, and display the values that are current inside your state object.

Creating, Updating, and Displaying State in a React Component

The last section showed how to use a proxy on your local machine and retrieve data. The fetch method, which is not part of React, was used to make a GET request of the server and return the results back to your component.

You now have the challenge of taking the results and displaying them on screen.

Each component in React has a concept of state. Inside the constructor function you will make a state object. This object will have properties that you will create and assign values to.

The two properties will be called boroughs and states. Each property will hold onto an array whose values you will set in a moment.

In this example, you will take the results of your API and use the built-in setState method to update the state you created. Your component should look like Listing 12-3.

Listing 12-3. boroughs.js Making an API Call and Displaying the Results on the Screen

```
import React, { Component } from 'react';

export class Boroughs extends Component {
constructor(props){
          super(props);
          this.state = {
          boroughs: [],
          states:[]
}
}

componentDidMount(){
   let boroughArray = [];
   let stateArray = [];
```

```
    fetch('/boroughs').then( (results) => {
        return results.json();
    }).then ( (resultJson) => {
        resultJson.map( (value, index) => {
                boroughArray.push(value.name);
                stateArray.push(value.state);
            });
        this.setState({
            boroughs: boroughsArray,
          state: stateArray
          });
      });
}

  createList(list){
  if (list.length !== 0) {
      const stateList = list.map( (value, index) => {
            return (<div> {value} </div>)
          });
        return stateList
    }
};
      render() {
        return(
                <div>
                    <div>
                <div>Boroughs:</div>
                <div> { this.createList(this.state.boroughs)} </div>;
                    </div>
                    <div>
                <div>States:</div>
                <div> { this.createList(this.state.states)} </div>;
                    </div>

                </div>
                    }

}
```

You import React and the `component` class the same way you import classes just using ES6. React components have the same format as an ES6 class. You extend the `component` class to give this class extra ability provided by the framework.

In this class, you use the `constructor` function. This function is called before the component is mounted. The first function you call is the `super` method. The reason for this is in case you want to do things like bind an event handler method to the current class.

You also have the ability to access the property called `state`. This is where you let React keep track of variables or objects. The framework can even let you know what the previous value was when it does get updated.

For now, you create these properties and assign each of them to be an empty array that you will update in a moment.

Next, you look at your lifecycle method `componentDidMount`. This gets executed when the component has been inserted into the DOM tree. This method is a good place to start working with any kind of outside data.

You create two local arrays and then use the `fetch` method. It will let you make a call to the remote server. Because of your proxy, a call to `/boroughs` will be redirected to your Node server, exactly like in the Angular application.

The `fetch` method allows you to chain a `then` method where you can call a function to process the results of the API call. Inside that function you take the results and return them back as a JSON object. With a new object returned, you chain a second `then` method and call another function. This function is used to loop though the data using the `map` method. When calling a function inside `map`, you iterate though each value and add them into the local array based on either the name or the state.

Once the loop is finished, you take both arrays and update the state of your application. Using the built-in `setState` method, you assign your array to the `state` properties.

Let's skip the next function for a moment and talk about the `render` function . Here is where React starts to process the HTML to be displayed on screen. The curly braces let React take variables and display them as valid HTML markup. From here you make a call to the `createList` method and pass over each property from your `state` object.

This brings you to the `createList` method. It accepts an argument called `list`, which is really a stand-in for either the `boroughs` or `states`, state in your React application.

The first thing the method does is make sure that the array that is getting passed does not have a length of zero, meaning that it cannot be an empty array. Once that has been determined, you loop though the array using map and return a list of HTML div elements with the value in the array. This list is returned back to the render method for the results to be displayed.

The function being called inside the render method will now generate HTML inside the browser. See Figure 12-3.

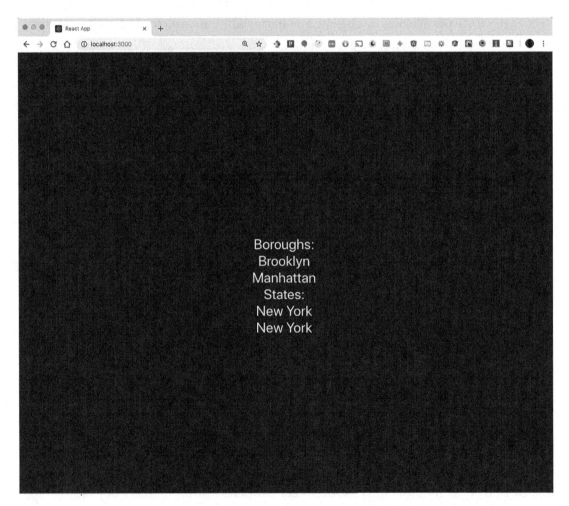

Figure 12-3. *Displaying the results on screen from the Node API*

Now that React has your results on screen, you can use CSS to display them. In the next section, you will add Bootstrap and update the layout of your application.

Adding Bootstrap to React

Just like Angular, there are a few ways to add Bootstrap to your React application. The way you are going to add Bootstrap is to use a project called reactstrap.

In install reactstrap, you need to go back to the command line at the base of your application and use NPM to install the library. At the command line, type

```
npm install bootstrap -save
npm install -save  reactstrap react react-dom
```

This will install both Twitter Bootstrap and reactstrap into your application. You can now use the same CSS classes to lay out the application. In order for your application to take advantage of having Bootstrap as part of the application, import it into the index.js file like this:

```
import 'bootstrap/dist/css/bootstrap.min.css'
```

Now without changing any of the JavaScript you can update the HTML part of your React app. See Listing 12-4.

Listing 12-4. Using reactstrap to Lay Out the Content of Your Component

```
<div className='container-fluid'>
    <div className='row'>
        <div className='col'>Boroughs:</div>
        <div className='col'>States:</div>
    </div>
    <div className='row'>
        <div className='col'> { this.createList(this.state.boroughs)} </div>;
        <div className='col'> { this.createList(this.state.states)} </div>;
    </div>
</div>
```

If you start the application again, the screen should look like Figure 12-4.

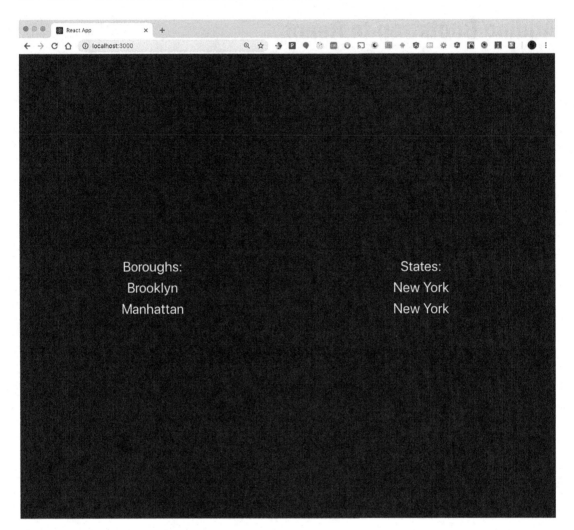

Figure 12-4. *Using reactstrap to get the same CSS classes as Bootstrap*

Your application now has information returning from the database and formatting using Bootstrap. The last section in this chapter will cover how to create a form and send the information to the database by way of the web service.

Posting Data from a React Application

You can retrieve data from a database and use Bootstrap to format the results into a table-like layout. Now you are going to change this layout by adding a HTML form so you can submit new data into the database and have a separate button to retrieve all the results after you have added new information into the database.

Some of the functions you used in earlier examples will still work in this exercise. However, this component will take on the responsibility of making a call to the server and then rendering the results in the browser.

Now that you have reactstrap added to your project, you can use it to make your form take shape. By importing components from the reactstrap library, they will be rendered in the browser using the formatting given by Bootstrap.

You will start by looking at the component as a whole and then break down all the individual pieces. See Listing 12-5.

Listing 12-5. boroughs.js Using reactstrap for Formatting Both Sending and Receiving Data from a Database

```
import React, { Component } from 'react';
import { Container, Col, Form, FormGroup, Label, Input, Button } from
'reactstrap';
import './css/boroughs.css';

export class Boroughs extends Component {
    constructor(props)} {
        super(props);
        this.state = {
          boroughs: [],
          states: [],
          boroughInput: '',
          stateInput: ''
        }
    };

    componentDidMount(){}

    createList = (list) => {
        if(list.length !== 0) {
            const itemList = list.map( (value, index ) => {
                return (<div> {value} </div>)
              });
            return itemList;
        }
    }
}
```

```
onSubmitForm = (e) => {
    e,prventDefault();
    fetch( '/boroughs', {method: "POST",
headers:{'Accept': 'application/json', 'Content-type':
'application/json'},
body: JSON.stringify({boroughName: this.state.boroughInput, state:
this.state.stateInput}) }).then((result) => {
  console.log(result);
    });
} )
}

onBoroughsUpdate = (event) => {
   this.setState({boroughInput: event.target.value});
}

onStatusUpdate = (event) => {
   this.setState({stateInput: event.target.valiue});
}

showResults = () => {
  let boroughArray = [];
  let stateArray = [];
   fetch('/boroughs').then( (results) => {
     return results.json();
  }).then( (resultJson) => {
   resultJson.map( (value, index ) => {
    boroughArray.push(value.name);
    stateArray.push(vaue.state);
   });
   this.setState({
         boroughs: this.createList(broughsArray),
         states: this.createList(stateArray)
   });
  });

}
```

```
render(){
    return(
        <Container className="borough-container">
            <Form className="form" onSubmit={this.onSubmitform}>
                <Col>
                    <FormGroup>
                    <Label>Add Name</Label>
                    <Input type="text" value=
                    {this.state.boroughInput} onChange=
                    {this.onBoroughUpdate) onBlur=
                    {this.onBoroughUpdate}/>
                    </FormGroup>
                </Col>
                <Col>
                    <FormGroup>
                    <Label>Add State</Label>
                    <Input type="text" value={this.state.
                    stateInput} onChange={this.onStateUpdte}
                    onBlur={this.onStateUpdate}/>
                    </FormGroup>
                </Col>
                    <Button>Submit</Button>
            </Form>
            <br/>
        <div>
        <div className="row">
            <div className="col">
                <button className="btn btn-primary" onClick=
                {this.showResults}>Show Results</button>
            </div>
        </div>
        <div className="row resultsPadding">
            <div className="col">
                Boroughs:
        </div>
```

```
        <div className="col">
            {this.state.boroughs}
        </div>

        <div className="col">
            States:
        </div>
        <div className="col">
          {this.state.states}
        </div>
      </div>

    </div>
      </Container>
      )
    }
}
```

This one class does a lot of work. It is helpful to take a good look and understand everything that it is doing. Let's start at the top and get into all the details.

At the very top, you import components that help make up your interface. You have encountered the React components before. The other components are coming from reactstrap. These components let you build forms, lists, and buttons that look the same as if you manually assigned the Bootstrap CSS classes to them.

The third line allows you to import CSS that is going to be used inside this component.

Inside the `constructor` function you create a few properties for your `state` object. The first two are arrays and the second two are strings.

You may notice that you are not using the lifecycle events in this example. In this case, you leave them blank.

The `createList` function works exactly the same way that it did in the last example. It generates a list of `div` elements based on the array that is passed over to it. One thing to note, since you are creating new `div` elements dynamically: React has an attribute called key. This is like giving a unique id to elements rendered by React. For more information, take a look at the official documentation (`https://reactjs.org/ docs/lists-and-keys.html`).

The onSubmitForm function first prevents the browser from refreshing by way of the preventDefault function. It then sends the values of what has been typed into the form fields to the database.

Using the fetch method, you first define the endpoint and then create an object that will inform fetch how it should pass the data over to the server.

This object contains a few properties. The first one is the type of REST call you want fetch to make. In this case, you are making a POST so you can update the database. The second property defines the headers that are going to be sent to the server. This lets the server know that you are about to send some JSON data over to it.

The third property is the data itself. It is sent over as the part of the body of the message that is being sent over to the server.

The data will be picked up by the server without needing to make any changes from the Angular example and will add a new record to the database.

The functions onBoroughsUpdate and onStatesUpdate perform the same type of action. In both cases, as someone is typing inside the input field the results are saved inside the state object. The onBlur event is executed when the user clicks something outside that text field. It will take the current value of the text field and assign it to the state object.

The showResults function performs the same way your previous componentDidMount function did. The only difference here is that when using the setState method you assign the results of the createList method.

Once you get to the render method, you get into most of the HTML elements that you see when the browser makes your UI visible. You can see, for example, the buttons respond to events like onClick and call functions that are defined in the component.

When running the application and the server, if you add something new to the database, you screen should look something like Figure 12-5.

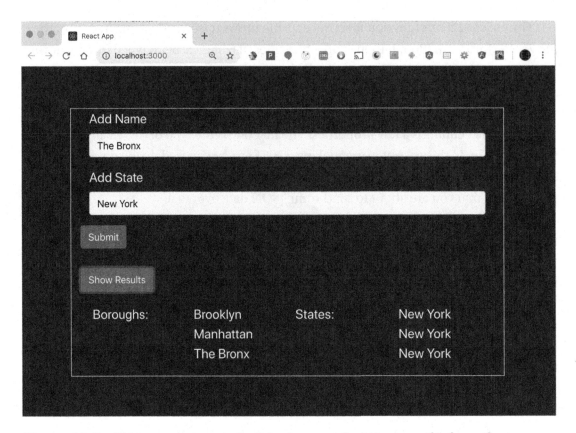

Figure 12-5. *Using reactstrap to build a form and retrieve results from the database*

Adding Strong Types to Your React Application

React does not enforce strong types in the way that Agular does using TypeScript. You can develop a React application and never need to enforce types in your JavaScript.

However, for large applications, it may be helpful to have type safety on your side and have JavaScript enforce datatypes.

Using Flow (https://flow.org/en/) in your React applications is optional, but it gives you the ability to have the compiler check the data types just like TypeScript or other languages like Java enforces types. It is also important to note that you can use React with TypeScript if you like (https://facebook.github.io/create-react-app/docs/adding-typescript).

In the previous examples using React, you used `create-react-app` to build your application. With this in mind, you can quickly add Flow to your application. At the command line, type

```
npm install --save-dev flow-bin
```

If you are using yarn, type

```
yarn add flow-bin
```

After installation, add this line to the scripts section of the `package.json` file:

```
"scripts":{
  "flow":flow
}
```

Now at the command line, create a file called `.flowconfig` by typing

```
npm run flow init
```

If you are using yarn, type

```
yarn flow init
```

With everything installed you can now add `//@flow` or `/* @flow */` to files where you want the compiler to start checking types. To check your file and understand where you need to add types at the command line, you can type

```
npm run flow check
```

This will look for each file with `//@Flow` added to it. The command line will show each file and where the types are expected.

You now need to understand how to add types in your code. In the next section, you will see how to do so.

Adding Types to Your React Code

Each React component has its own internal state. The `state` object keeps track of values that you want the component to be aware of all the time. All of the properties assigned to the `state` object can be assigned strong types. You can define these types before defining the class. It should look like this:

```
type State = {
  boroughs: Array<string>,
  states: Array<string>,
  boroughInput: string,
  stateInput: string
}
```

This example defines the datatypes. You learned how an array works; here you define that the datatype is going to be an array, but you also define what type of data will be used inside that array. In this instance, `boroughs` and `states` will both hold an array. The main difference here is that it will be an array with strings as values.

If you add a different data type to that array, the compiler will throw an error because here you told it exactly what to expect.

The other two properties represent the text field that you use to add new data to the database. In this case, they are both are typed as a string.

React also allows you to set the data type for properties in the same way. Once the types are set, you can apply them to the component:

```
export class Boroughs extends Component<Props, State>{ }
```

Now if you assign a number to something that has been assigned a string, the compiler will throw an error.

When working with functions, the syntax is just like TypeScript. Parameters can have types set so when you pass data over to the function they need to be of that type. Here is an example:

```
function doMath(num1: number, num2: number){
    return num1 + num2;
  }
doMath(5,2);
```

You can also assign types to variables:

```
let username: string = "Hack One";
const accountNumbber: number = 11220;
var currentTime: string = "Time to make the donuts";
```

While this is an overview, it gives you insight into how to make sure you are working with the correct types when it comes to your data. Flow is optional, but it's easy to add it to existing code a file at a time or to add type checking on every file as you are developing a new project.

Summary

This chapter explored some of the basics of the React library. While you can put all the pieces together yourself, React has a command line interface that will let you put an application together quickly.

One of the ideas that React and Angular share is the concept of lifecycle events. These events are built into the framework to let you know what stage the component is currently in.

The first example used the componentDidMount event. When this event was triggered, it made a call to the database.

The other examples brought in Bootstrap for layout and the ability to style things like buttons and forms.

The final example used a form that sent a POST to the database and added new information. You also added a button that made a GET request and displayed all the updated information from the database.

While there are some differences between Angular and React, there are also some very similar ideas surrounding concepts like lifecycle events.

Flow is similar to TypeScript in that you can enforce type safety in your JavaScript application. While TypeScript as a language is a superset of JavaScript, Flow lets you take your current JavaScript and apply types to it.

One of the advantages to using Flow is that you can find errors at compile time. In addition, you can make sure that your functions are both receiving and returning the right kind of data so they can perform properly. A good example of this is when you want to update a string or calculate a value.

You have been able to develop applications on your local computer by taking advantage of frameworks and your knowledge of JavaScript. The next chapter will show you how to take an application and deploy it to a live server for other people to see.

CHAPTER 13

JavaScript and Static Deployment

You have done a lot of development on your local machine, working with JavaScript directly in the browser and then using frameworks like Angular and React to develop applications that rely on data from the server. Now that you have an understanding of what it is like to work with larger applications, you can move these applications from your laptop to a server to be seen by everyone.

For this example, you are going to use JSONPlaceholder as the source of your data and focus on the front-end development.

In earlier chapters of this book I discussed how to use Git as a way of keeping track of all the changes that your application will go though over time. While this is important, Git does not help with letting others see the site as a finished product.

What you need is a way to automatically deploy your code to a remote server where visitors can then see all your hard work in action.

This chapter will first describe what a static site is and how to use a service like Netlify to move your code from a service like GitHub to a live server.

Developing an Angular Application and Connecting It to GitHub

Static websites are really all the parts that make the front end work. In this case, it's the HTML, JavaScript, CSS, images and any other media that you need to deliver the site to the browser.

All of the interaction with the database will be handled by a different server that will respond to all API calls.

For this example, you will make a basic Angular application. It will be just like your other example.

© Russ Ferguson 2019
R. Ferguson, *Beginning JavaScript*, https://doi.org/10.1007/978-1-4842-4395-4_13

Make sure you add the Angular router in your project. At the command line, type

```
ng new static-app
```

This code puts together your bare Angular application. With your application created, now make a photos component and an albums component:

```
cd static-app
ng generate module media
ng generate component media/photos
ng generate component media/albums
```

Finally, create a service that will retrieve data for both components:

```
ng generate service /media/services/service
```

Once all of these components and services have been added to the project, you can add Bootstrap, but in a different way than you did in the past. Here you are going to use a project called ng-bootstrap (`https://ng-bootstrap.github.io`). It will give you all the features of Bootstrap without needing to install libraries like jQuery.

At the command line, install ng-bootstrap:

```
npm install  --save bootstrap
npm install --save @ng-bootstrap/ng-bootstrap
```

With Bootstrap added, you need to make sure the Angular application can take advantage of it. There are two ways of doing this. One is to install the main module into the root of your application. The other is to add per module only the modules that you need to make that module work.

To keep your application simple, open `app.module.ts`. Here you can import NgbModule into the application and add it to the `imports` array.

Once that is finished, open the `angular.json` file. In the styles section, add these lines in order to pick up all the CSS that is built into Bootstrap to work inside your application:

```
"styles": [
  "src/styles.sass",
 "node_modules/bootstrap/dist/css/bootstrap.min.css",
"node-modules/font-awesome/css/font-awesome.min.css"
 ]
```

Your application is now at a good stage to back it up. If you have an account with a site like GitHub or BitBucket, you can make a new repository for your code.

In the case of GitHub, open source projects can be hosted for free. Click the Create repository button and name your project as `static-site`. See Figure 13-1.

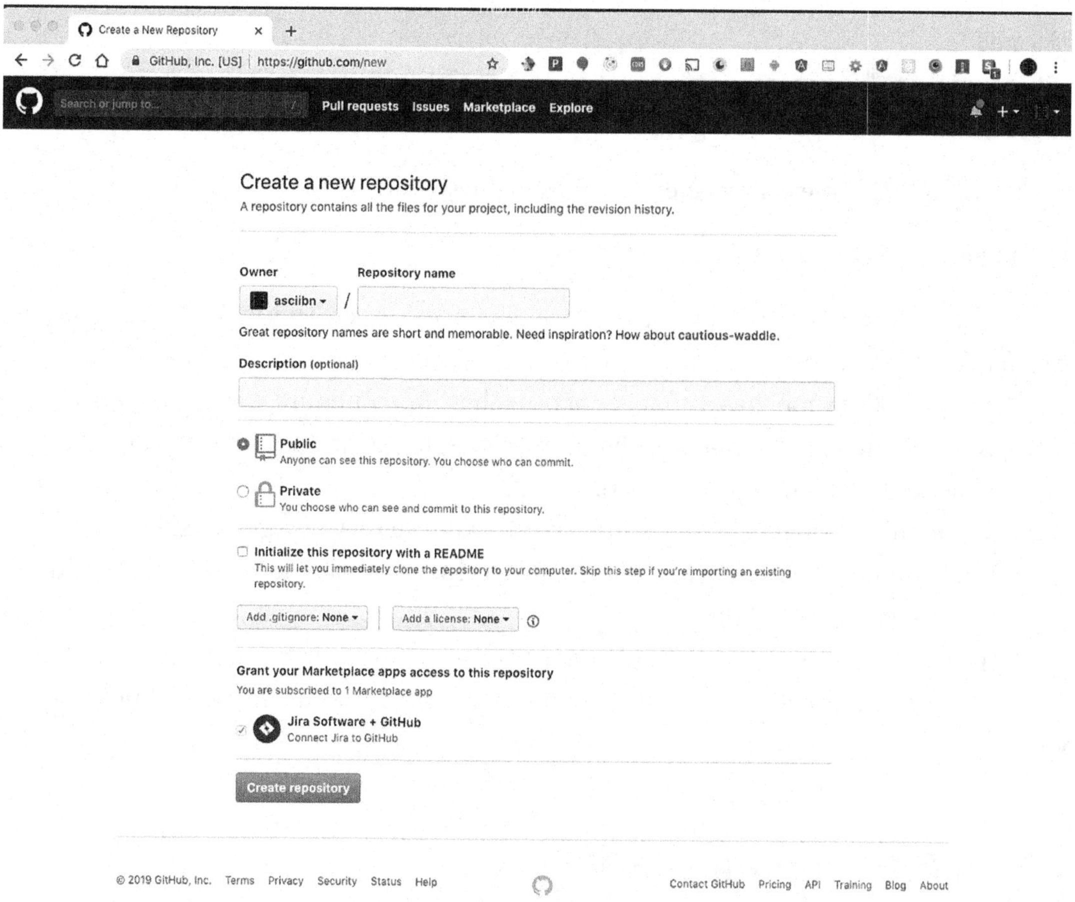

Figure 13-1. *Creating a public repository using GitHub*

Once the repository has been created, you will get instructions to connect the files on your computer to the remote server.

When you used the CLI to create your site, Angular created a local repository on your machine. This is great for keeping track of the changes in your code but isn't helpful if you want to work on this project with other people. Another benefit of having your code on a remote server is for automatic deployment. You can grab the latest version of the site and move the compiled code to a live server.

When using the command line to connect to GitHub you may need to configure an SSH key. This will allow you to log into GitHub and have control over your remote repositories. For information about how to set that up, refer to GitHub at `https://help.github.com/articles/adding-a-new-ssh-key-to-your-github-account/`.

At the command line, add the ability to connect to your remote server:

```
git add .
git commit -m "first commit"
git remote add origin git@github.com:USER-NAME/static-site.git
```

The next line copies or "pushes" the files to the server:

```
git push -u origin master
```

You should now have a copy of the site on a remote server. This will also give you a visual reference to changes that happen to the files over time.

Git as a workflow tool has a concept of `branches`. Branches are just a copy of the entire project. This lets you make individual changes to the project. These changes can then be merged into the master branch.

This chapter is not a complete tutorial on workflow with Git; a good explanation with visual references can be found at `www.atlassian.com/git/tutorials/comparing-workflows/gitflow-workflow`.

Now that you have both your application and your repository put together, the next section will let you use the Angular router and Bootstrap to create the two sections of your site.

Using the Angular Router

The last section had you create a brand-new Angular application with the router added. You then added Bootstrap components and connected the whole project to a public repository on GitHub.

This section will show you how to use the Angular router to create a menu for the site. As you make updates, you will keep track of them using Git.

This example will show a very quick way of using the Angular Router. A more detailed explanation can be found at `https://angular.io/guide/router`.

To create your simple routing functions, add some code to `app.module.ts`. First, you import two items from the @angular/router path. Import RouteModule and Routes. The line should look like this:

```
import { RouterModule, Routes } from '@angular/router';
```

You also need to import your two visual components, PotosComponent and AlbumsComponent:

```
import { PotosComponent } from '../media/photos/photos.component';
import { AlbumsComponent } from '../media/albums/albums.component';
```

Remember to take these newly imported components and add them to the declarations array inside the app.module.ts file:

```
@NgModule ({
declarations: [
    AppComponent ,
    PhotosComponent,
    AlbumsComponent
  ]
})
```

After that, make an array of objects to represent your routes. This array has the datatype of Routes and is assigned to a variable called appRoutes. Route objects have predetermined properties. These properties tell Angular how the route should work.

Some of the properties are

- path: The path that matches the URL

- patchMatch: Regular expression to match the URL

- component: The component you want to see when the route is resolved

- redirectTo: Where you need to redirect when a path has been found

- data: Any data that needs to be assigned to that route

- children: Any subroutes, for example /borough/id

Your example will just take advantage of two of these properties, path and component.

Your route will look like this:

```
const appRoutes: Routes = [
      {path: 'photos', components: PhotoComponent}.
      {path: 'albums', components: AlbumsComponent}
]
```

Having these routes worked out is important. You can make them more sophisticated and have them deal with issues like if someone does not have a URL that the Angular application will recognize. You can set a default route.

With your array set up, you can pass it to the `RouterModule` that will be inside the `imports` array:

```
imports: [
 RouterModule.forRoot(appRoutes)
]
```

To make sure your updates are working, you can add a few buttons to the application that will update the routes when clicked.

Open the `app.component.html` file. Here you have the default welcome page that was generated when you built the application. You need to remove all this code and add something new.

In previous examples, you used Bootstrap to lay out your page. This example will use the same skills. You start with a container and then define the rows and columns that will make up the page. Then you need to add a custom element defined by Angular that will handle your routes.

Listing 13-1 shows what the updated page should look like.

Listing 13-1. The Updated Page

```
<div class="container-fluid">
   <div class="row">
     <div class="col-12">
        <h3>Static Site</h3>
     </div>
   </div>
```

```
<div class="row">
    <div class="col-1">
      <button class="btn btn-primary" routerLink='/photos'>Photos</button>
    </div>
    <div class="col-1">
      <button class="btn btn-primary" routerLink='/albums'>Albums</button>
    </div>

  </div>
</div>
<router-outlet></router-outlet>
```

This is the same type of layout that you used in other examples. One big difference is how you use the buttons. The button adds a property called routerLink. The value is passed to the router and when a match has been found, Angular loads the component in the area where the router-outlet element is on the page. See Figure 13-2.

Figure 13-2. *The Angular Router lets you navigate though a single page application*

After the files have been saved, the browser should update and your buttons should be active with the ability to change the location in the browser and load the appropriate component.

With the files updated and your site offering new functionality, now is a good time to save the current state of your files and save them in your repository.

To see which files have been changed, at the command line, type

```
git status
```

You can see a list of the files that you worked on to get this far. Next is to tell Git to add these files into what Git thinks of a staging area:

```
git add angular.json
git add package-lock.json
git add package.json
git add src/app/app.component.html
git add src/app/app.module.ts
git add src/app/media/media.module.ts
```

Now that you have your files in staging, it is time to make your commit. This is where you have Git save the change so it now has a way to compare how the files were to what they are like now. In addition to making a commit, you can also add a message that describes the changes at this stage.

To make a commit, type

```
git commit -m "Angular routing added to the application"
```

The -m in this line tells Git that you want to add a message with your commit. It is followed by the message in quotes.

Your commit has been made but all the changes are saved on the local machine. What you need to do is have these changes saved on the remote server. This is done by using the push command to share the updates with the remote repository on GitHub:

```
git push
```

You may be asked to input your GitHub password. The updates are then sent to your repository, with the changes now visible on the website. See Figure 13-3.

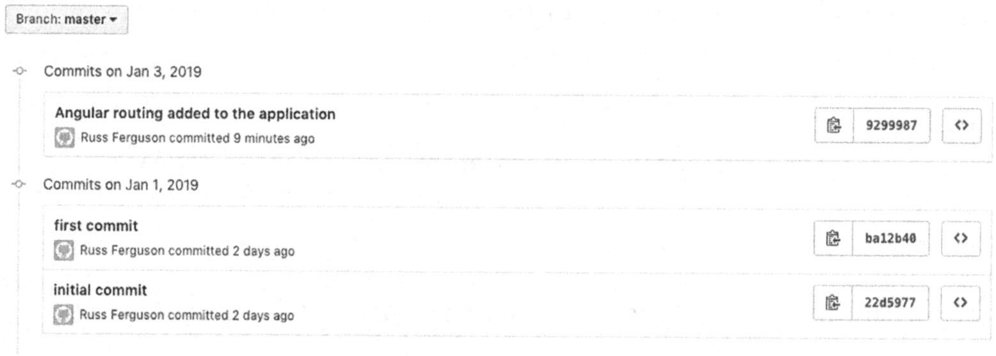

Figure 13-3. *Changes to the application over time*

You have been able to add navigation to your application and keep track of your changes over time. Now you can see the changes both locally and in your GitHub repository.

The next section will show you how to pull data for each section using Angular services.

Using Angular Services

Services in Angular let you inject or use the same code into multiple components. This gives you a separation of work where the component can receive data and display it and the service can make the request of a remote service and parse the results.

In order for a service to have the ability to make calls to remote services, the main application needs to have `HttpClientModule` imported and added to the `imports` array. Open the `app.module.ts` file and import the module:

```
import { HttpClientModule } from '@angular/common/http';
```

Now you can direct your service to make remote calls. Open `service.service.ts`. Here you can import the `HttpClient` library to make your call:

```
import _{ HttpClient } from '@angular/common/http';
```

Using the `constructor` function, you make your `http` instance:

```
constructor ( private http: HttpClient ) { }
```

Finally, you add two methods, one to get all of the photos and the other to get all of the albums:

```
getAlbums() {
   return this.http.get('https://jsonplaceholder.typicode.com/albums ');
}

getPhotos() {
   return this.http.get('https://jsonplaceholder.typicode.com/photos ');
}
```

One of the nice things about services is that you can use them in multiple components. In this next example, you inject a service into your component. It works the same way in both components. Each component needs to import the service and create an instance inside the constructor.

The next example shows how to retrieve photos using this service inside the PhotosComponent. The service can also be used inside the AlbumsComponent in the same way.

The service object has been created inside the constructor. When the component runs the lifecycle method ngOnInit, the service will then run the method getPhotos and return the results back to the component. In the case of the AlbumsComponent, it will run the method getAlbums.

Part of the PhotosComponent code should look like this:

```
constructor (private: service: ServiceService) {}
ngOnInit() {
   this.service.getPhotos().subscribe( (results) => {
      this.photoResults = results;
   });
}
```

The HTML template can now be updated with the results from the web service. Use the *ngFor directive to loop through the array of results to show the title and the thumbnail image returning from the service. See Listing 13-2.

Listing 13-2. The HTML Template

```
<div class="container-fluid">
    <div *ngFor="let photo of photosResult" class="row">
        <div class="col-1">
            <p>Title</p>
        </div>
        <div class="class=col-6">
            <p>{{photo.title}}</p>
        </div>
        <div class="col-2">
            <img src="{{photo.thumnailURL}}">
        </div>
    </div>

</div>
```

This example shows how to create a for loop through your results and get the details. These details will generate all of the HTML needed to create all the rows and columns needed. One of the important things to point out is the generation of images. Because the URL is being generated by the results of the web service call, you can apply that value to the source of the image and that image will be rendered in the browser. See Figure 13-4.

Figure 13-4. *The rendered results of calling the photos API*

Your site now has routes that you can go to directly by either using the buttons or typing in the URL. These routes render components that use the same service class to make a call to your data source and render the results on screen.

You made updates to a few files to make this work. Now is a good time to keep track of these changes. Go back to the command line to use the same git commands to save the current state of your application.

First, check the status of the changed files:

```
git status
```

If all the files that have been changed are in the same folder, for example the src folder, you can use a shortcut to stage them all:

```
git add src
```

If the updated files are in other folders, you must add the path to those files. If you like, you can check the status again to see if all the files are now in the stash.

Next, you make a commit:

```
git commit -m "Routing and Service added"
```

Finally, you push the changes to the server:

```
git push
```

Like the previous example, this will now copy all the files from your local machine to the GitHub server, with the history of all the changes made to these files.

You now have both a working site and a backup of the files your site needs to work. With your source code on GitHub, you can now connect it to a service that will deploy your application and make it available to the world.

The next section will discuss how to connect to Netlify, a service designed to deliver the front end of an application, also called a static site.

Deploying a Static Site to Netlify

Netlify (`www.netlify.com/`) is one of a series of services that try to make deploying your site fairly painless. There is a free tier for someone working on a personal site. Once signed up, a developer can use a domain name developed by the service, one they already own, or buy a domain that they can manage on their own though the service.

Deploying a site gives you the ability to point to your own source code currently living in GitHub. Let the service copy the files, build the project, and push the final results to a server with a public address where everyone can see your site.

On the top right corner of the browser window is a button called New site from Git. Click it. The next screen asks for the location of your source code. This is why it was important to get it off the local machine and onto a service like GitHub. Select the service you are using. Netlify will ask you for permission to access your account on the other service. Once permission is granted, you can then point to the repository that you created to hold your static site. See Figure 13-5.

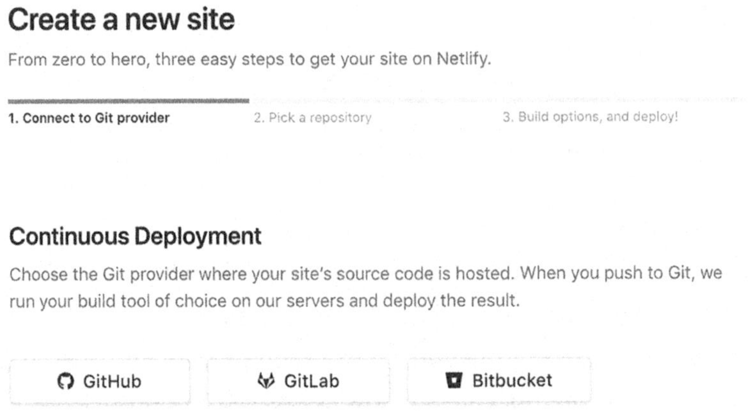

Create a new site

From zero to hero, three easy steps to get your site on Netlify.

1. Connect to Git provider   2. Pick a repository   3. Build options, and deploy!

Continuous Deployment

Choose the Git provider where your site's source code is hosted. When you push to Git, we run your build tool of choice on our servers and deploy the result.

⬡ GitHub   𝖄 GitLab   🪣 Bitbucket

Figure 13-5. *When creating a new site, you need to point to the code repository*

When selecting the repository that has all of your code, Netlify will ask what branch you want to deploy. In this case, you only have one branch so it's *master*. It will also ask what command it should run to compile the application. In this example, you are using Angular so the command is `ng build`. Remember that you need to build the site so that all the code can be turned into JavaScript that the browser can understand. The last thing it needs to know is where to find the finished site. This is in the `dist/static-app` folder. See Figure 13-6.

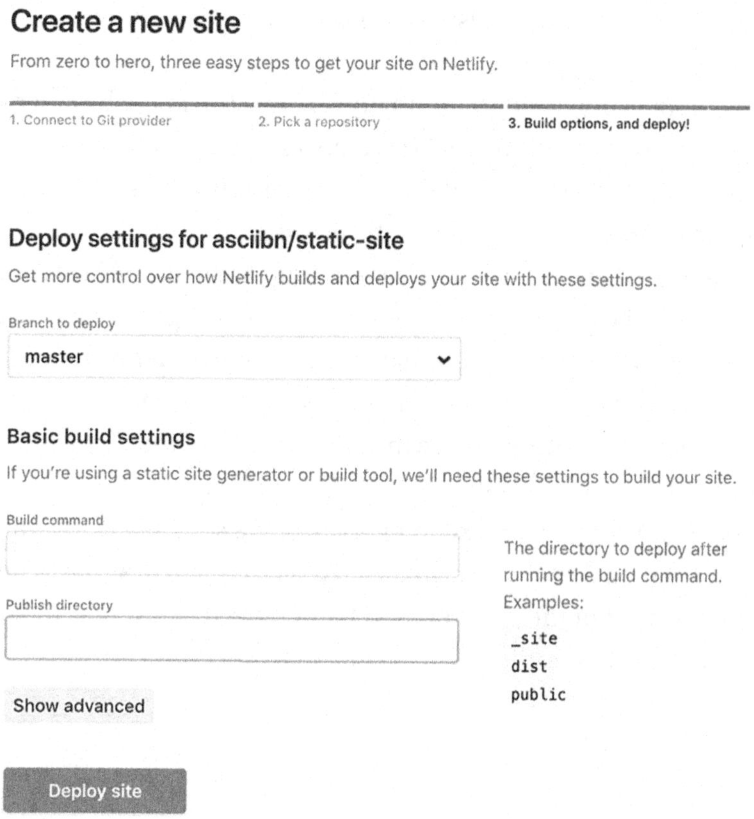

Create a new site

From zero to hero, three easy steps to get your site on Netlify.

1. Connect to Git provider   2. Pick a repository   **3. Build options, and deploy!**

Deploy settings for asciibn/static-site

Get more control over how Netlify builds and deploys your site with these settings.

Branch to deploy

```
master                                        ⌄
```

Basic build settings

If you're using a static site generator or build tool, we'll need these settings to build your site.

Build command

```
```

Publish directory

```
```

Show advanced

The directory to deploy after running the build command. Examples:

```
_site
dist
public
```

Deploy site

Figure 13-6. *Directing Netlify to the build the site and indicating where the finished files will be found*

Give it a few minutes and Netlify will give you a URL where you can see your live site. You can then look at the URL in your browser and even send the URL to friends where they can see the live version of your site.

Now that you have your account and project working, you can use some of the other features provided by the service, like the ability to set up a custom domain or add security to your site.

Summary

This chapter covered on a very basic level the production process of building a web application. Developers work on the site on their local machines, retrieve data from a remote source, and display the results. The files that make up the project are saved in a repository with a history of the changes over time. Finally, the files are moved to a service where they are compiled, and the finished version is posted to a server where the site now lives.

Your Angular application used routes to update the URL in the browser and display certain components on demand. You also created a service that was responsible for making requests of the web service and sending the results back to the component so that the component could render results in the browser.

Over time it is a good idea to save the current state of the files. This is done with version control software like Git. Using tools like Git not only gives you a history of how the files changed over time, but you can share the files with other people when the project is in a public repository. As you work on your project, when you feel that you are in a good place, that's a good time to save the current state of the files with Git. There are very good tutorials at `www.atlassian.com/git/tutorials`.

After developing the project and keeping track of the source code, it was time to deploy the application. In this chapter, you used a service called Netlify. There are other ways to deploy your site, but the point of this chapter was to show how to take the source code and automatically deploy the finished version to a server.

Index

A

addEventListener method, 57
alert() function, 7
   JavaScript syntax example, 6
Angular framework
   borough class, 158
   CLI to create service, 144–146
   CLI to update service, 147–150
   components, 141–144
   developing, 137–140
   FormsModule, 156
   installation, 136
   modules, 141–142
   passing information to node, 159–162
   proxy, creation, 150–154
   twitter bootstrap, 154–155
   updating list-borough-component,
      156–157
Application programming
      interface (API), 84
apply method, 52–53, 76
Array
   definition, 39
   example, 39
   filter method, 42
   forEach method, 42
   getting length of, 40
   reduce method, 43
   using loops, 41
Arrow function, 47–48

B

Babel tool, 111
Bitbucket, 21
Boroughs, 128, 167

C

Client side development
   babel.js, 111–113
   HTML Webpack plugin, 113–114
   module bundlers (Webpack), 106–109
   Sass/SCSS features, 115–118
   webpack-dev-server, 110
Code execution, 5, 7
Command line interface (CLI), 135
Command line tools, 100
componentDidMount function, 170
console.clear() function, 85
console.log method, 8, 54, 84
core objects, 9

D

Document object, 9, 37–38

E

Event bubbling, 57
Event propagation
   bubbling, 62–63
   custom events, creation, 65–66

203

Printed in the United States
By Bookmasters